Example

key word
rhyming sound

hole
-ole

rhyme family

mole   pole   role   sole   stole   vole   whole

Sometimes there are several words from one rhyme family which rhyme with words from another rhyme family.

Example

-ole rhymes with *-oal*
coal   foal   goal

-ole also rhymes with *-oll*
poll   roll   scroll   stroll   troll

And sometimes there are words that rhyme with the key word but have a different spelling pattern

Example

Other words that rhyme with *mole*

bowl   soul

Rhymes

There are lots of rhymes throughout the dictionary. You can use these rhymes as a starting point for rhymes of your own.

A jaguar from Zanzibar
Learned to sing and to play the guitar.
Now he's a famous movie star
And drives around in a sports car.

Indexes

The dictionary has two indexes. The A-Z index on page 146 lists every word in this dictionary. The key words are printed in bold type. This index will tell you the page where you will find the rhyming words you are looking for.

The Index of Rhyming Sounds on page 143 lists every rhyming sound in this dictionary. You can look up the sound that you want to make rhymes with and go straight to the key word in the main part of the book.

Activities

There is an activities section on page 130. These suggest things you can do to practise making up rhymes and writing rhyming poems.

These are the features of the dictionary:

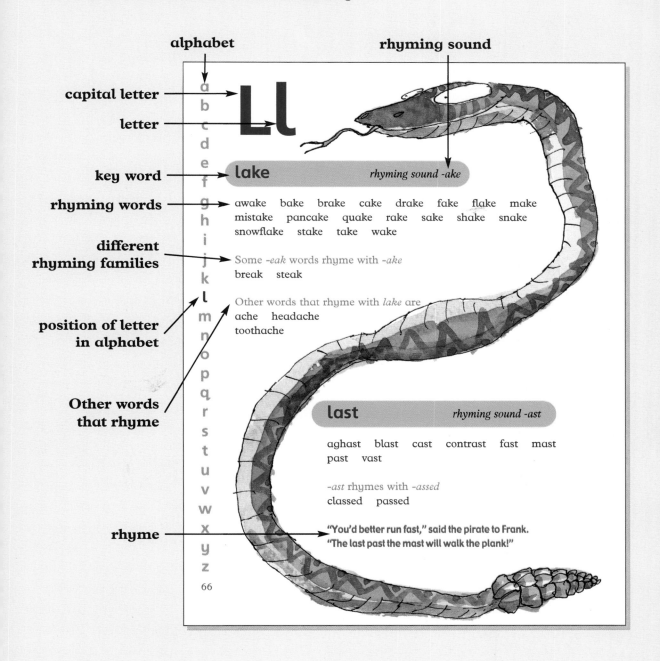

alphabet

capital letter

letter

rhyming sound

a
b
c
d
e
f
g
h
i
j
k
l
m
n
o
p
q
r
s
t
u
v
w
x
y
z

Ll

lake   *rhyming sound -ake*

awake   bake   brake   cake   drake   fake   flake   make
mistake   pancake   quake   rake   sake   shake   snake
snowflake   stake   take   wake

Some *-eak* words rhyme with *-ake*
break   steak

Other words that rhyme with *lake* are
ache   headache
toothache

last   *rhyming sound -ast*

aghast   blast   cast   contrast   fast   mast
past   vast

-ast rhymes with *-assed*
classed   passed

**"You'd better run fast," said the pirate to Frank.
"The last past the mast will walk the plank!"**

key word

rhyming words

different
rhyming families

position of letter
in alphabet

Other words
that rhyme

rhyme

66

7

Aa

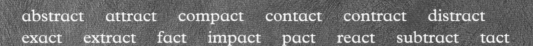
act — *rhyming sound -act*

abstract   attract   compact   contact   contract   distract
exact   extract   fact   impact   pact   react   subtract   tact

-act rhymes with -acked

backed   backpacked   backtracked   cracked   hijacked
humpbacked   lacked   packed   quacked   sacked   smacked
snacked   stacked   tracked   unpacked   whacked

air — *rhyming sound -air*

chair   despair   fair   flair   hair   lair   mid-air   pair
repair   stair   unfair

-air rhymes with -are

aware   bare   beware   blare   care   compare   dare   declare
fare   glare   hare   mare   nightmare   prepare   rare   scare
share   snare   software   spare   square   stare

-air rhymes with -aire

billionaire   millionaire   solitaire

Other words that rhyme with *air*
bear   pear   prayer   swear   their
there   wear   where

OXFORD

This book is to be returned on or before the last date below.
You may renew the book unless it is requested by another borrower.
THANK YOU FOR USING YOUR LIBRARY

OXFORD
UNIVERSITY PRESS

Great Clarendon Street, Oxford OX2 6DP

Oxford University Press is a department of the University of Oxford.
It furthers the University's objective of excellence in research, scholarship,
and education by publishing worldwide in

Oxford   New York

Auckland   Cape Town   Dar es Salaam   Hong Kong   Karachi
Kuala Lumpur   Madrid   Melbourne   Mexico City   Nairobi
New Delhi   Shanghai   Taipei   Toronto

With offices in

Argentina   Austria   Brazil   Chile   Czech Republic   France   Greece
Guatemala   Hungary   Italy   Japan   South Korea   Poland   Portugal
Singapore   Switzerland   Thailand   Turkey   Ukraine   Vietnam

Oxford is a registered trade mark of Oxford University Press
in the UK and in certain other countries

British Library Cataloguing in Publication Data

Data available

ISBN   hardback 10 digit: 0 19 911191 X
13 digit: 978 0 19 911191 6

ISBN   paperback 10 digit: 0 19 911192 8
13 digit: 978 0 19 911192 3

1 3 5 7 9 10 8 6 4 2

Typeset in Great Britain by Macwiz

Printed in Italy by G. Canale & C. spa

OXFORD
Junior
Rhyming
Dictionary

John Foster
Illustrated by
Melanie Williamson
Rupert Van Wyk

How to use this dictionary

You can use this dictionary to help you to find words that rhyme. When you want to find the rhymes for a particular word, the A-Z index on page 146 will help you to find the right page in the dictionary.

You can also use the dictionary to learn how to spell words that belong to the same rhyming family. You will find an index of rhyming sounds on page 143.

The alphabet

The key words in this dictionary are listed in alphabetical order.
There is an alphabet line down the side of each page to help you to find your way round the dictionary.

Key words

A key word is a word that you use very often. In this dictionary, the key words are in **bold**. You can look up a key word and find a list of other words that rhyme with it.

Rhyme family

A rhyme family is a family of words that end with the same rhyming sound and have the same spelling pattern.

Each key word belongs to a rhyme family. You will find the rhyming sound after the key word.

Ride on the Ghost Train if you dare.
Feel the spiders as they brush your hair.
Shiver at the gleaming eyes that stare.
Cringe as you pass the vampire's lair.

Ride on the Ghost Train **if you dare!**

a
b
c
d
e
f
g
h
i
j
k
l
m
n
o
p
q
r
s
t
u
v
w
x
y
z
9

ant
rhyming sound -ant

currant   descendant   elegant   elephant   pant
rant   restaurant   scant

arm
rhyming sound -arm

alarm   charm   farm   harm

-arm rhymes with *-alm*
calm   palm

ask
rhyming sound -ask

bask   cask   flask   mask   task

Bb

bang
rhyming sound -ang

boomerang   clang   fang   gang   hang
overhang   pang   rang   sang   slang
sprang   tang   twang

As the midnight bell rang,
The werewolf bared its fang
And **sprang**

bank
rhyming sound -ank

blank   clank   crank   dank   drank   frank
lank   plank   prank   rank   sank   shrank
spank   stank   tank   thank   yank

beach
rhyming sound -each

bleach   each   peach   preach   reach   teach

-each rhymes with *-eech*
beech   screech   speech

My sister gave a loud **screech**
As she bit through the slug in her peach.

belt *rhyming sound -elt*

celt dwelt felt knelt melt pelt
spelt welt

Another word that rhymes with *belt* is
dealt

big *rhyming sound -ig*

dig earwig fig gig jig oil rig pig
rig sprig swig twig whirligig wig

bike *rhyming sound -ike*

alike dislike hike like pike spike strike trike

bird *rhyming sound -ird*

ladybird third

Other words that rhyme with *bird*
absurd blurred heard herd nerd preferred
purred stirred whirred word

black
rhyming sound -ack

attack back backpack bareback crack flapjack
hack haystack horseback jack knack
lack lumberjack pack piggyback
quack rack rucksack sack
shack slack smack snack
soundtrack stack tack
track unpack whack

Other words that rhyme
with *black*

anorak kayak mac maniac
plaque tarmac yak

Mr Black, Mr Black,
Please can we have our
     football back?
You can pass it through
     the window.
It'll fit through the crack.
Oh, don't be a spoilsport, Mr Black.
Please give us our football back.

a
b
c
d
e
f
g
h
i
j
k
l
m
n
o
p
q
r
s
t
u
v
w
x
y
z

bone

rhyming sound -one

alone   clone   cone   drone   lone   megaphone   ozone   phone
postpone   prone   stone   timezone   throne   tombstone   tone
trombone   xylophone   zone

-one also rhymes with *-own*
blown   flown   grown   known   own   shown   sown   thrown

Other words which rhyme with *bone*
groan   loan   moan   sewn

**"I feel ill," said the king and gave a groan,
when he saw the bill for his mobile phone.**

boot

rhyming sound -oot

beetroot   hoot   loot   reboot   root
scoot   shoot   toot

-oot also rhymes with *-ute*

acute   brute   chute   cute   dilute   dispute   execute   flute
minute   mute   parachute   pollute   salute   substitute

Other words that rhyme with *boot*

fruit   newt   suit

An elephant in a parachute.

A koala bear playing the flute.

A penguin whizzing down a chute.

And a hippopotamus in a suit.

15

boss
rhyming sound -oss

across   albatross   candyfloss   cross   floss
gloss   loss   moss   toss

bounce
rhyming sound -ounce

announce   flounce   ounce   pounce   pronounce
trounce

bridge
rhyming sound -idge

fridge   midge
porridge   ridge

Oh dear! I'm in trouble.
I shouldn't have blown
that bubblegum bubble!

brother
rhyming sound -other

another   mother   other   smother

bubble
rhyming sound -ubble

rubble   stubble

-ubble also rhymes with *-ouble*
double   trouble

a
b
c
d
e
f
g
h
i
j
k
l
m
n
o
p
q
r
s
t
u
v
w
x
y
z

Cc

car *rhyming sound -ar*

afar   ajar   bar   caviar   cigar   far   guitar   jaguar
jar   scar   spar   star   tar   tsar

Other words that rhyme with *car*
are   aha   baa   bizarre   ha   ha-ha   ma   pa

A jaguar from Zanzibar
Learned to play the bass guitar.
Now he's a famous movie star
And drives round in a racing car!

cart   *rhyming sound -art*

apart   art   chart   dart   depart   heart   part
smart   start   tart

catch   *rhyming sound -atch*

attach   batch   detach   hatch   latch   match
mis-match   patch   scratch   snatch   thatch

cave
rhyming sound -ave

behave   brave   crave   forgave   gave   grave
heatwave   knave   microwave   pave   rave   save   shave
shockwave   slave   wave

"Behave!" said the queen to the knave.
"Or you'll drive me to an early grave!"

coat
rhyming sound -oat

afloat   boat   float   gloat   goat   moat   oat
stoat   throat

-oat rhymes with *-ote*
devote   dote   note   promote   quote
remote   rote   vote   wrote

cook

rhyming sound -ook

book brook crook hook look mistook nook rook
shook took

My hands shook
When I saw the evil look
In the eyes of Captain Hook
As he le**apt** from the
page of my book.

At dawn I saw a unicorn.
I watched it grazing on the lawn,
The sunlight glinting on its horn.

corn   *rhyming sound -orn*

acorn   adorn   born   forlorn   horn   morn   scorn
shorn   sworn   thorn   torn   unicorn   worn

-orn rhymes with *-awn*
airborne   borne   dawn   drawn   fawn   frogspawn
lawn   leprechaun   pawn   sawn   yawn

cow
rhyming sound -ow

allow bow bow-wow brow eyebrow how meow now
ow! pow row sow vow wow

-ow rhymes with some words ending in *-ough*
bough plough

crab
rhyming sound -ab

cab dab drab fab flab grab jab kebab lab
nab scab slab stab

You mustn't try to grab
A very bad-tempered crab.
For if you do,
I'm telling you,
Its pincers will give you a jab.

Anon

crash

rhyming sound -ash

ash bash cash clash dash flash gash gnash hash
lash mash rash sash slapdash slash smash splash
thrash trash whiplash

Lightning flash

Thunder crash

Winds lash

Trees thrash

Raindrops splash

Storms smash!

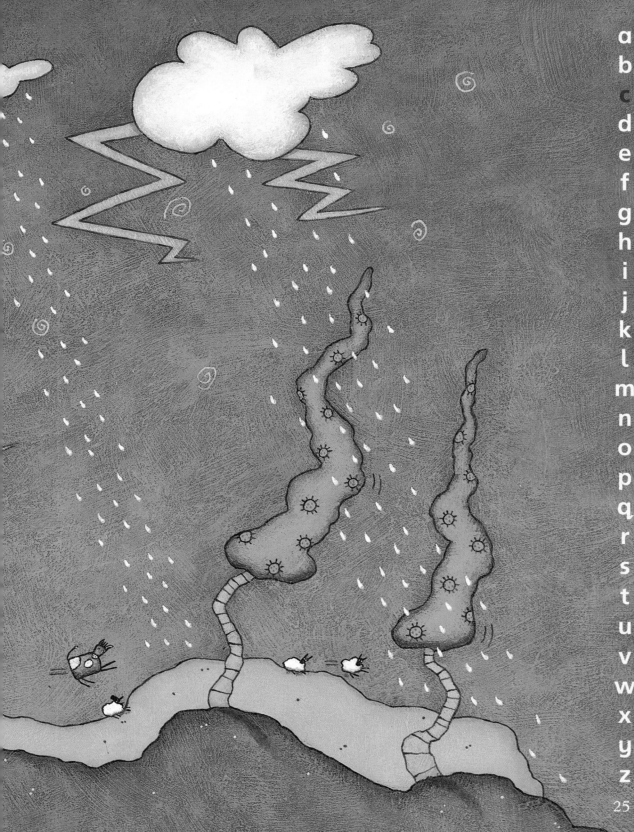

crept
rhyming sound -ept

accept   adept   except   inept   intercept   kept   slept
swept   wept

Other words that rhyme with *crept*
leapt   stepped

I slept in, so I crept in,
But Miss saw me, so I was kept in.

Dd

dad   *rhyming sound -ad*

bad   clad   fad   glad   had   lad   mad
nomad   pad   sad

Another word that rhymes with *dad* is
add

**"You're not a bad lad," said dad.
"But your music drives me mad!"**

dance   *rhyming sound -ance*

advance   chance   entrance   France   glance   lance
prance   stance   trance

27

dark

rhyming sound -ark

aardvark   ark   bark   embark   hark   landmark
lark   mark   park   remark   shark   spark

"My bite is worse than my bark," said the shark.
"With my teeth I leave my mark!"

dinner
rhyming sound -inner

beginner   inner   sinner   spinner
thinner   winner

dog
rhyming sound -og

agog   bog   clog   cog   flog   fog   frog   grog
hog   jog   log   slog

-og also rhymes with *-ogue*
catalogue   monologue

dream
rhyming sound -eam

beam   cream   daydream   gleam
icecream   scream   seam   steam
stream   team

-eam also rhymes with *-eem*
redeem   seem   teem

Other words that rhyme with *dream*
extreme   scheme   supreme   theme

a
b
c
d
e
f
g
h
i
j
k
l
m
n
o
p
q
r
s
t
u
v
w
x
y
z

dress   *rhyming sound -ess*

address   bless   chess   confess   cress   depress   distress
excess   express   guess   happiness   helpless   impress
kindness   less   loneliness   mess   oppress   possess   press
princess   progress   stress   success   tress   unless

Another word that rhymes with *dress* is
yes

Nicola Nicholas couldn't care less.
Nicola Nicholas tore her dress.
Nicola Nicholas tore her knickers.
Now Nicola Nicholas is knickerless.

duck   *rhyming sound -uck*

buck   chuck   cluck   luck   muck   pluck
struck   stuck   suck   truck   tuck   yuck

dust   *rhyming sound -ust*

adjust   bust   crust   disgust
gust   just   must   rust
thrust   trust

a b c d e f g h i j k l m n o p q r s t u v w x y z

Ee

ear
rhyming sound -ear

appear   clear   dear   disappear   fear
gear   hear   near   rear   shear   smear
spear   tear

-ear rhymes with *-eer*
beer   buccaneer   career   cheer   deer   engineer   jeer
leer   mountaineer   musketeer   peer   pioneer   sheer
sneer   steer   veer   volunteer

-ear rhymes with *-ere*
atmosphere   here   mere   persevere
revere   severe   sincere

Other words that rhyme with *ear*
cashier   cavalier   frontier   gondolier
pier   souvenir   weir

We all gave a cheer
as the wizard made our teacher
disappear.

east
rhyming sound -east

beast   feast   least   yeast

-east rhymes with *-eased*
ceased   creased   deceased   greased
increased   released

elf
rhyming sound -elf

bookshelf   herself   himself   itself
myself   self   shelf   yourself

end
rhyming sound -end

ascend   attend   bend   blend   defend   depend
descend   extend   friend   intend   lend   mend   offend
pretend   recommend   send   spend   suspend   tend   trend

Here lies Charlotte Cul-de-Sac,
A most annoying friend,
She used to drive me round the bend
Until she came to a dead end.

ever
rhyming sound -ever

clever   forever   however   never   sever   whatever
whenever   wherever   whichever   whoever

a b c d e f g h i j k l m n o p q r s t u v w x y z

33

Ff

face
rhyming sound -ace

ace brace commonplace disgrace embrace
fireplace grace lace misplace pace place
race replace shoelace space trace

-ace also rhymes with *-ase*
base bookcase case chase database
staircase suitcase

There was a young girl called Grace
Whose nose spread all over her face
She had very few kisses
And the reason for this is
There wasn't a suitable place.

Anon

find

rhyming sound -ind

behind   bind   blind   grind   kind   mind   remind
rewind   rind   unkind   wind

-ind rhymes with *-ined*

dined   fined   lined   mined   pined   whined

Another word that rhymes with *find* is
signed

When
you stand
in a
queue,
it's not
kind
to remind
anyone
you're
behind
that
you're
behind
their
behind.

fire

rhyming sound -ire

admire bonfire desire dire empire hire inquire inspire
quagmire spire squire tire umpire vampire wire

Other words that rhyme with *fire*
choir flyer friar fryer higher
liar pyre tyre

Here lies a foolish young squire
Who was the most terrible liar.
He collapsed one day
And passed away
From the heat of his pants on fire!

first
rhyming sound -irst

thirst

Other words that rhyme with *first*
burst   cursed   nursed   rehearsed   worst

fish
rhyming sound -ish

dish   perish   punish   rubbish   selfish
squish   swish   vanish   wish

**Three selfish shellfish each had a wish.
The wish each selfish shellfish wished
was a selfish shellfish wish.**

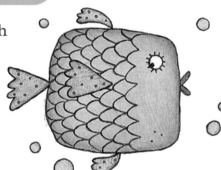

five
rhyming sound -ive

alive   arrive   dive   drive   hive   jive   live   revive
strive   survive

Another word that thymes with *five* is
I've

flag
rhyming sound -ag

bag   brag   crag   drag   gag   hag   lag   nag   rag
sag   snag   stag   swag   tag   wag   zigzag

a
b
c
d
e
f
g
h
i
j
k
l
m
n
o
p
q
r
s
t
u
v
w
x
y
z

food   *rhyming sound -ood*

brood   mood

-ood also rhymes with *-ewed*
brewed   chewed   mewed   screwed   slewed   viewed

-ood also rhymes with *-ooed*
booed   boo-hooed   cooed   mooed   shampooed   shooed
tattooed   wooed

-ood also rhymes with *-ude*
altitude   attitude   crude
exclude
gratitude   include
intrude   nude   rude
solitude

-ood also rhymes
with *-ued*
argued
barbecued   glued
pursued
rescued   sued

fox

rhyming sound -ox

box   cox   ox   pox

-ox rhymes with *-ocks*

blocks   clocks   docks   flocks   frocks   knocks   locks   mocks
rocks   shocks   socks   stocks

Goldilocks wears pretty frocks
But I wish she'd change her   smelly socks.

freeze

rhyming sound -eeze

breeze   sneeze   squeeze   wheeze

-eeze rhymes with *-ees*
agrees   bees   chimpanzees   degrees   dungarees   fees
flees   frees   knees   referees   sees   toffees   trees

-eeze also rhymes with *-ease*
disease   ease   please   tease

Other words that rhyme with *-eeze*
cheese   chimneys   donkeys   fleas   keys   monkeys
peas   seas   seize   skis   teas   these   trapeze

Chimpanzees in dungarees
Swing with ease on the trapeze,
While bees on skis
Struggle to juggle packs of peas.

a b c d e f g h i j k l m n o p q r s t u v w x y z

43

fur

rhyming sound -ur

blur   occur   slur   spur

-ur rhymes with *-ir*
fir   sir   stir

-ur also rhymes with *-er*
badger   her   otter
prefer   slipper   tiger

Other words that rhyme with *fur*
purr   were   whirr

Always call a tiger "Sir"
And do not try to stroke his fur
For tigers are well known to Grrr!

Gg

gate

rhyming sound -ate

appreciate   ate   calculate   celebrate   concentrate   confiscate
crate   create   date   debate   decorate   educate   estate
estimate   exaggerate   fascinate   fate   frustrate   grate   hate
investigate   irritate   Kate   late   mate   operate   plate   rate
separate   skate   slate   state

-ate also rhymes with *-ait*
bait   wait

Other words that rhyme with *gate*
eight   fete   great   straight   weight

Elephant! Elephant!
Don't try to skate.
The ice is too thin,
It won't bear your
weight...

Too late!

girl
rhyming sound -irl

swirl   twirl   whirl

-irl rhymes with *-url*
curl   furl   hurl   unfurl

Other words that rhyme with *girl*
earl   pearl

glass
rhyming sound -ass

brass   bypass   class   grass   pass   trespass

grape
rhyming sound -ape

agape   ape   cape   drape   escape   gape
landscape   scrape   shape   tape

grub

rhyming sound -ub

club   cub   dub   hub   hubbub   pub   rub   scrub   shrub
snub   stub   tub

A grubby grub sat in a tub
And sang as he had a good scrub:

"I'm a scrub-a-grub, rub-a-dub grub!"

Hh

hairy — *rhyming sound -airy*

airy   dairy   fairy

-airy rhymes with *-ary*
canary   contrary   Mary   scary   vary   wary

hand — *rhyming sound -and*

and   band   brand   expand   gland   grand   land
sand   stand   strand   understand

-and rhymes with *-anned*
banned   canned   fanned   manned   planned
scanned   spanned   tanned

hat

rhyming sound -at

acrobat   aristocrat   at   bat   brat   cat   chat   combat   fat
flat   gnat   habitat   mat   pat   pit-a-pat   rat   rat-a-tat-tat
sat   spat   splat   that   vat   wombat

There was a young fellow called Matt
Who wanted to look like a cat
His feet were like paws
With retractable claws
And whiskers grew out of his hat.

Anon

hen

rhyming sound -en

amen   Ben   den   fen   glen   Ken   Len   men
pen   ten   then   when   wren   yen

Another word that rhymes with *hen* is
again

hit

rhyming sound -it

admit   bandit   biscuit   bit   circuit   culprit   exit   fit   flit
grit   habit   it   kit   knit   lit   nit   omit   orbit   outfit   permit
pit   quit   rabbit   sit   spit   split   summit   twit   visit   wit

a b c d e f g h i j k l m n o p q r s t u v w x y z

hole

rhyming sound -ole

casserole   console   dole   mole   pole   role
sole   stole   tadpole   vole   whole

-ole rhymes with *-oal*
coal   foal   goal   shoal

-ole also rhymes with *-oll*
poll   roll   scroll   stroll   troll

Other words that rhyme with *hole*
bowl   control   soul

Old King Cole scored   a very fine **goal**
A very fine goal scored he.
A TV poll reckoned King Cole's goal
Was the best you'd ever see.

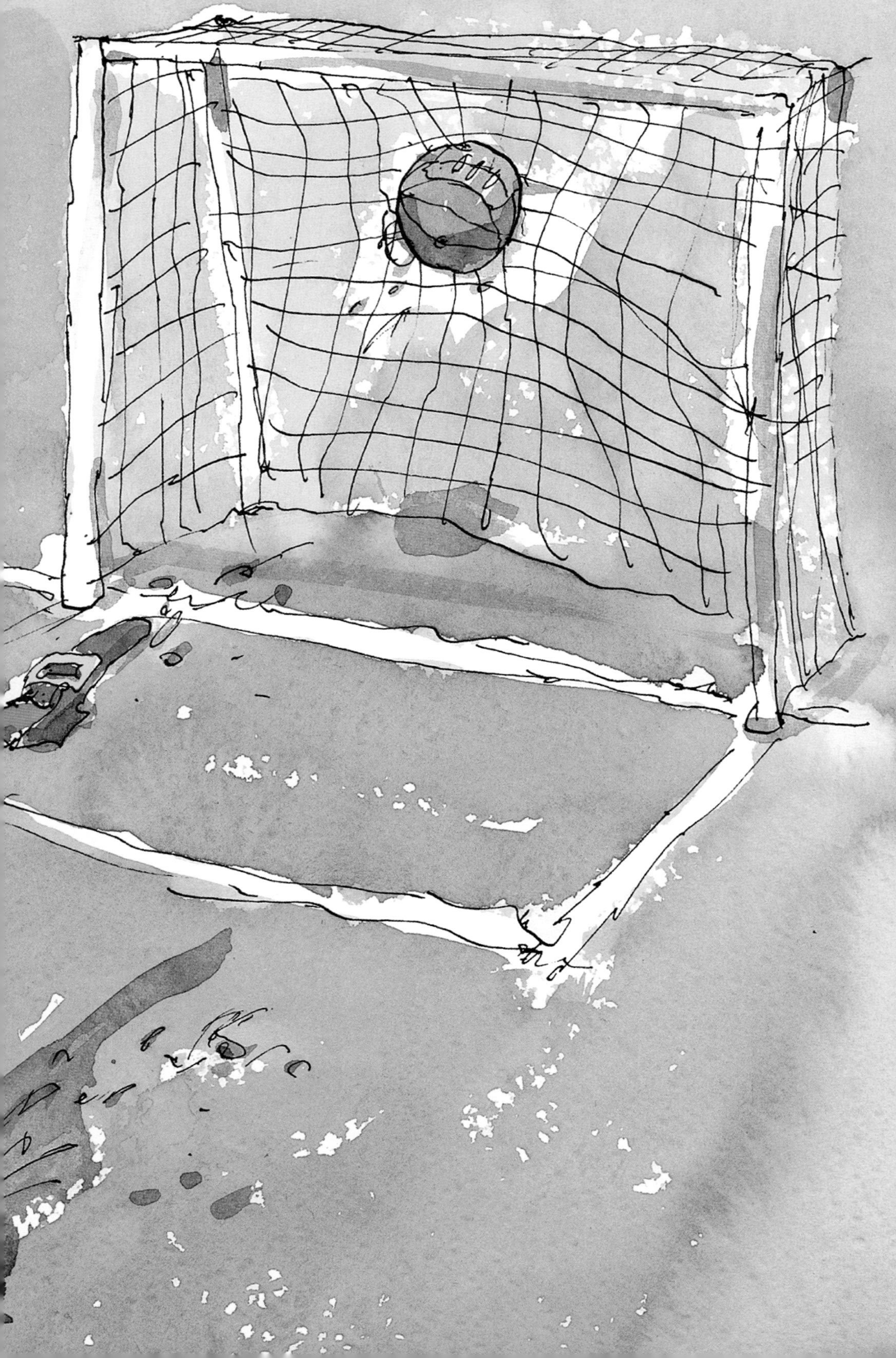

a b c d e f g **h** i j k l m n o p q r s t u v w x y z

honey

rhyming sound -oney

money

-oney rhymes with *-unny*

bunny   funny   runny   sunny

I eat my peas with honey.
I've done it all my life.
It makes the peas taste funny.
But it keeps them on the knife.

Anon

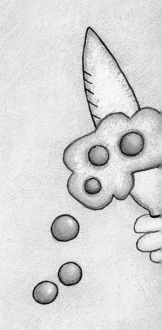

hood *rhyming sound -ood*

childhood   deadwood   driftwood   falsehood   good
neighbourhood   stood   understood   wood

-ood rhymes with *-ould*
could   should   would

hoop *rhyming sound -oop*

coop   droop   loop   nincompoop
scoop   sloop   snoop   stoop
swoop   troop   whoop

-oop rhymes with *-oup*
group   soup

house *rhyming sound -ouse*

louse   mouse   spouse

A mouse and his spouse doing cartwheels round the house.

hunt
rhyming sound -unt

blunt　grunt　punt　runt　shunt　stunt

Another word that rhymes with *hunt* is
front

hut
rhyming sound -ut

but　chestnut　cut　doughnut　glut　gut
jut　nut　rut　shut　strut　tut-tut

Another word that rhymes
with *hut* is
putt

Ii

ice

rhyming sound -ice

advice   dice   lice   mice   nice   price   rice   sacrifice   slice
spice   splice   trice   twice   vice

The three blind mice said,
"It's not very nice
Of the farmer's wife
To want to slice
Our tails off with her carving knife!"

Other words that
rhyme with *ice*
paradise
precise

ill

bill   brill   chill   drill   fill   frill   gill   grill   hill   Jill   kill
mill   pill   quill   shrill   sill   skill   spill   still   swill   thrill
till   will   windmill

-ill rhymes with *-il*

daffodil   fulfil   nil   Phil   tranquil   until

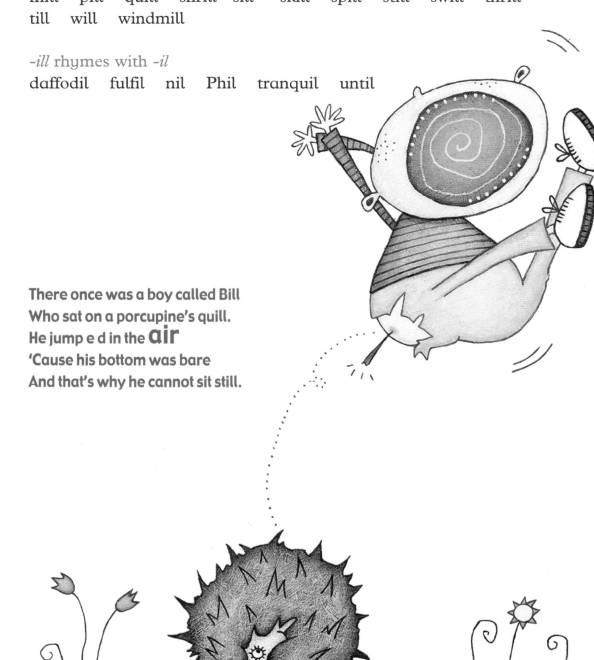

There once was a boy called Bill
Who sat on a porcupine's quill.
He jump e d in the **air**
'Cause his bottom was bare
And that's why he cannot sit still.

imp
rhyming sound -imp

chimp   crimp   limp   primp   scrimp
shrimp   skimp   wimp

ink
rhyming sound -ink

blink   brink   chink   clink   drink   kink   link   mink
pink   rink   shrink   sink   slink   stink   think   wink   zinc

itch
rhyming sound -itch

ditch   glitch   hitch   pitch   snitch
stitch   switch   twitch   witch

-itch rhymes with *-ich*
ostrich   rich   which

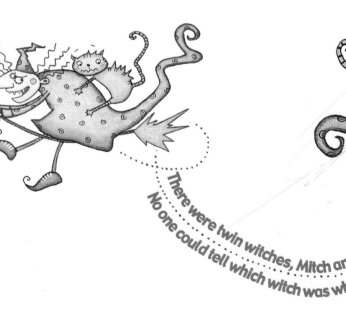

There were twin witches, Mitch and Titch.
No one could tell which witch was which.

Jj

jam   *rhyming sound -am*

am   cram   dam   exam   gram   ham
Pam   pram   program   ram   Sam   scam
scram   sham   slam   swam   tram   wham
wigwam   yam

Another word that rhymes with *jam* is
lamb

jet   *rhyming sound -et*

alphabet   basket   bet   bracelet   bucket   carpet   clarinet
cricket   duet   fidget   forget   fret   gadget   get   helmet
internet   jacket   let   magnet   met   net   pet   pocket
puppet   regret   rocket   secret   set   ticket   trumpet   upset
vet   wet   yet

-et also rhymes with *-eat*
sweat   threat

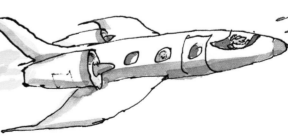

-et also rhymes with *-ette*
baguette   cassette   courgette   launderette
omelette   serviette

Another word that rhymes with *jet* is
debt

job
rhyming sound -ob

blob bob cob gob hob hobnob knob lob mob
rob snob sob throb

jug
rhyming sound -ug

bug chug drug dug glug hug humbug lug mug
plug rug shrug slug smug snug thug tug

A slimy slug drank from a jug.
A grubby bug drank from a mug.

Then the slug gave the bug a hug!

jump
rhyming sound -ump

bump clump dump frump goosebump hump
lump plump pump rump slump stump
thump trump

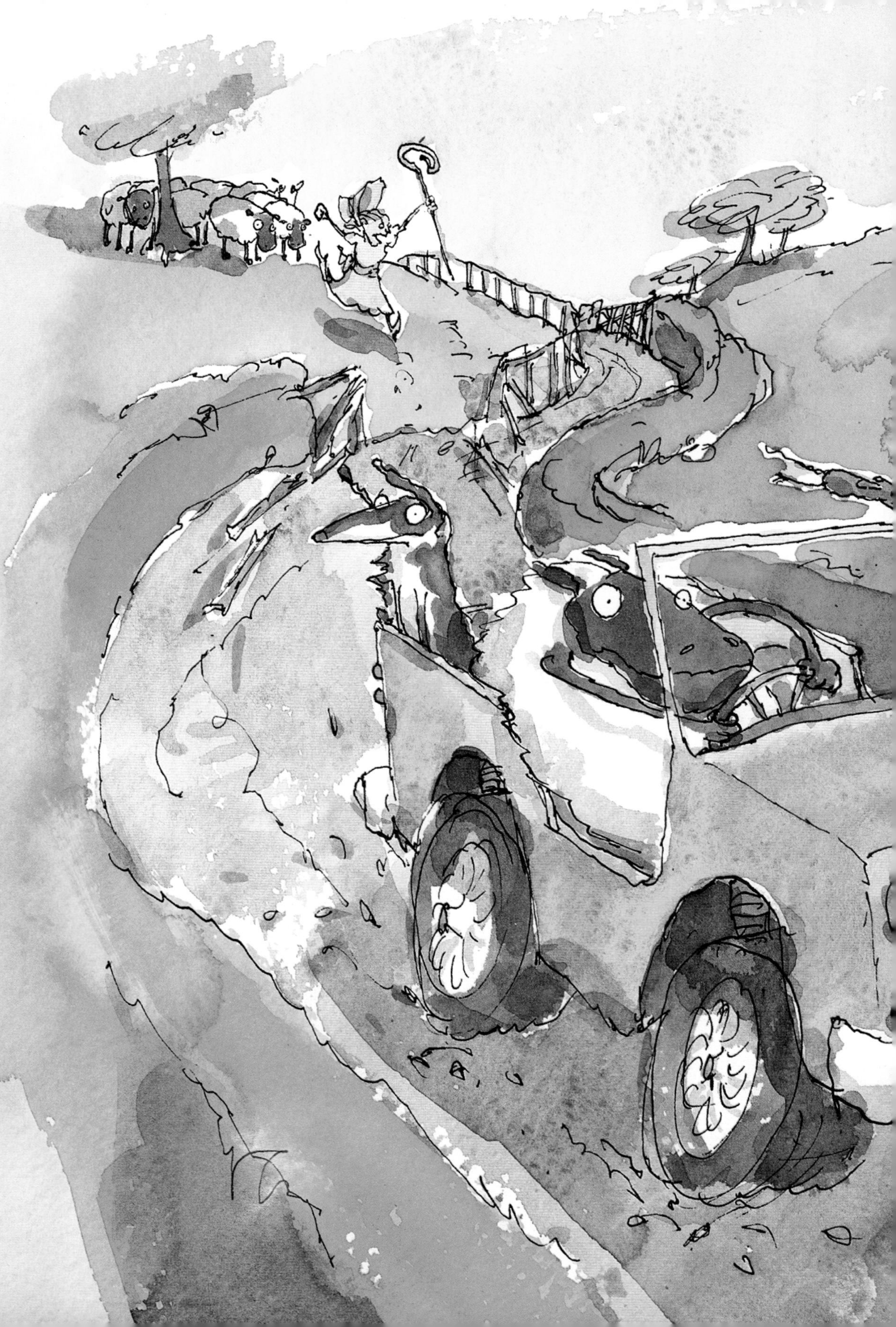

a b c d e f g h i j **k** l m n o p q r s t u v w x y z

Kk

keep

rhyming sound -eep

asleep   beep   bleep   cheep   creep   deep   jeep
peep   seep   sheep   sleep   steep   sweep   weep

-eep rhymes with *-eap*
cheap   heap   leap   reap

I'm a runaway sheep.
I stole the keys to Bo Peep's jeep
While she was lying fast asleep
Get out of my way! **Beep! Beep!**

a b c d e f g h i j k l m n o p q r s t u v w x y z

63

king

rhyming sound -ing

boring   bring   ceiling   cling   ding   fling   ping   ring
sing   sling   spring   sting   string   swing   thing   wing
wring   zing

When the bee gave the king a sting
The king did a highland fling.
So his arm ended up in a sling.

kiss

rhyming sound -iss

amiss   bliss   dismiss   hiss   kiss   miss

Other words that rhyme with *kiss*
liquorice   office   practice   promise   service   this

I'll be good, Mum, just promise me this:
You won't try to give me a kiss
In the playground. Just give it a miss!

knock

rhyming sound -ock

block   clock   crock   dock   flock   frock   lock   mock
rock   shock   sock   stock   tick-tock

Ll

lake
rhyming sound -ake

awake bake brake cake drake fake flake make
mistake pancake quake rake sake shake snake
snowflake stake take wake

Some *-eak* words rhyme with *-ake*
break steak

Other words that rhyme with *lake* are
ache headache
toothache

last
rhyming sound -ast

aghast blast cast contrast fast mast
past vast

-ast rhymes with *-assed*
classed passed

"You'd better run fast," said the pirate to Frank.
"The last past the mast will walk the plank!"

leg
rhyming sound -eg

beg   dreg   Greg   keg   Meg   nutmeg   peg

Another word that rhymes with *leg* is
egg

lid
rhyming sound -id

bid   did   forbid   grid   hid   liquid   kid   pyramid   quid
rapid   rid   rigid   skid   slid   squid   stupid   timid   undid

I slid back the bolt and undid the locks
To see what lay hid in the secret box.

a
b
c
d
e
f
g
h
i
j
k
l
m
n
o
p
q
r
s
t
u
v
w
x
y
z

light
rhyming sound -ight

bright　delight　fight　flight　fright　knight　midnight
might　night　outright　playwright　plight　right　sight
slight　stagefright　tight　tonight　twilight　upright　uptight

-ight rhymes with *-ite*
appetite　bite　dynamite　excite　ignite　invite　kite　mite
polite　quite　recite　site　spite　sprite　unite　website
white　write

Other words that rhyme with *light*
byte　height

When Dwight Wright had stagefright,
Mrs Wright said, "Don't get uptight, Dwight,
It'll be all right on the night."

After the first night, Dwight Wright
Said, "It went all right.
You were quite right, Mrs Wright."

lord

rhyming sound -ord

afford   chord   cord   ford   record   sword

-ord rhymes with *-oard*

aboard   board   cardboard   hoard   keyboard
scoreboard   skateboard

-ord also rhymes with *-ored*

adored   bored   explored   ignored   scored   snored   stored

Other words that rhyme with *lord*

abroad   applaud   award   broad   horde   poured   reward
roared   soared   toward   ward

The crowd roared and began to applaud
As the young lord drew his sword,
Slew the monster and claimed the reward.

love
rhyming sound -ove

above   dove   glove   shove

lunch
rhyming sound -unch

brunch   bunch   crunch   hunch   munch   punch   scrunch

lung
rhyming sound -ung

bung   clung   dung   flung   hung   rung   slung   sprung
strung   stung   sung   swung   wrung

Other words that rhyme with *lung*
among   tongue   young

Mm

map *rhyming sound -ap*

bap   cap   chap   clap   flap   gap   kidnap   lap   nap
overlap   rap   sap   scrap   slap   snap   strap   tap
trap   unwrap   wrap   yap   zap

On the Clip Clop Clap
All the Flops flip flap
And the Bongles boogle in the breeze.
The Sniggers snip snap
The Trotters trip trap
And the Somersaults sniff and sneeze
The Somersaults sniff and sneeze.

meat
rhyming sound -eat

beat   bleat   cheat   defeat   eat   feat   heat   neat
peat   pleat   repeat   retreat   seat   treat   wheat

-eat rhymes with *-eet*
discreet   feet   fleet   greet   meet   parakeet   sheet
sleet   street   sweet

-eat also rhymes with *-ete*
athlete   compete   complete   concrete   delete

Pete dressed up in a sheet
And went round the street
Knocking on doors
Saying, **"Trick or treat?"**

But at number thirty four
Pete got more
Than he bargained for,
When a troll opened the door!

So Pete beat a hasty retreat.

merry
rhyming sound -erry

berry   cherry   ferry   Terry

Other words that rhyme with *merry*
bury   very

middle
rhyming sound -iddle

diddle   fiddle   griddle   riddle   twiddle

Hey diddle riddle
The first is in first
The rest is in middle!

mist   *rhyming sound -ist*

cyclist   fist   insist   list   resist   tourist   twist   wrist

-ist rhymes with *-issed*
dismissed   hissed   kissed   missed

mix   *rhyming sound -ix*

fix   matrix   phoenix   six

-ix rhymes with *-icks*
bricks   broomsticks   chicks   clicks   flicks   gimmicks
kicks   licks   matchsticks   nicks   picks   pricks   sticks
ticks   tricks

The ghost of the conjuror said,
"I'm really in a fix.
The problem is the audience
Sees right through all my tricks."

moon   *rhyming sound -oon*

afternoon   baboon   balloon   bassoon
cartoon   croon   harpoon   honeymoon
lagoon   macaroon   maroon   noon
platoon   raccoon   saloon   soon
spoon   swoon   tycoon   typhoon

A baboon in a saloon playing a tune on a bassoon.

-oon rhymes with *-une*

dune   fortune   June   Neptune   prune   tune

Another word that rhymes with *moon* is
strewn

mud   *rhyming sound -ud*

bud   cud   dud   scud   spud
stud   sud   thud

Other words that rhyme with
mud
blood   flood

mum   *rhyming sound -um*

chum   drum   glum   gum   hum
plum   rum   scrum   scum   slum
strum   sum   swum   tum   yum
yum-yum

-um rhymes with *-umb*

crumb   dumb   numb   plumb   succumb
thumb

Other words that rhyme with *mum*
become   come   some

Nn

name — rhyming sound -ame

became   blame   came   fame   flame   frame   game
lame   same   shame   tame

-ame rhymes with *-aim*
acclaim   aim   claim   exclaim   maim

I am the wizard's dragon.
I speak with tongues of flame.
I am the wizard's dragon.
Firesnorter is my name.

neck   *rhyming sound -eck*

beck   check   deck   fleck   peck   speck   wreck

Other words that rhyme with *neck*
cheque   Czech   discotheque   high-tech   trek

**"Just let me check," said the vampire.
"I think there's a speck
Of blood on your neck."**

nettle   *rhyming sound -ettle*

fettle   kettle   settle

-ettle rhymes with *-etal*
metal   petal

nine

airline brine combine define dine divine fine line
mine pine recline shine shrine spine swine twine
valentine vine whine wine

-ine rhymes with *-ign*
design resign sign

It sent a shiver down my spine
When I received a valentine,
Saying, "I think you are divine"
'Cause it was signed 'Frankenstein'!

nose

rhyming sound -ose

chose   close   expose   hose   pose   prose   propose   rose
suppose   those

-ose rhymes with *-ows*

arrows   bellows   blows   bows   bungalows   crows   elbows
flows   glows   grows   knows   meadows   mows   rows
shadows   shows   slows   snows   sows   stows   throws   tows

-ose also rhymes with *-oes*

foes   goes   hoes   toes   woes   oboes
volcanoes   tiptoes   dominoes   potatoes

-ose also rhymes with *-os*

radios   stereos   videos

Other words that rhyme with *nose*

bulldoze   doze   froze   sews
UFOs

**When the winter wind blows
An icicle grows on the scarecrow's nose
And it looks just like Pinnochio's!**

Oo

oak   *rhyming sound -oak*

cloak   croak   soak

-oak rhymes with *-oke*
awoke   bloke   broke   choke   coke
joke   poke   provoke   smoke   spoke
stroke   woke   yoke

Other words that rhyme with *oak*
folk   yolk

oil   *rhyming sound -oil*

boil   broil   coil   foil   recoil   soil   spoil
toil   turmoil

-oil rhymes with *-oyal*
loyal   royal

Another word that rhymes
with *oil* is
gargoyle

old

behold   bold   cold   fold   gold   hold   marigold   scaffold
scold   sold   told

Other words that rhyme with *old*
bowled   cajoled   consoled   controlled   mould   patrolled
polled   rolled   soled   strolled

"Behold!" said the wizard
And he conjured a room full of gold.
But my blood ran cold,
When he warned,
"My secrets must never be told."

out

rhyming sound -out

about   blackout   bout   clout   dugout   hideout
knockout   lookout   lout   pout   rout   scout
shootout   shout   snout   spout   sprout   stout
throughout   trout   without

Other words that rhyme with *out*
doubt   drought

owl

rhyming sound -owl

fowl   growl   howl   prowl   scowl   yowl

-owl rhymes with *-owel*
bowel   towel   trowel   vowel

Another word that rhymes
with *owl* is
foul

Pp

page

rhyming sound -age

age   cage   engage   enrage   outrage   rage
rampage   sage   stage   teenage   upstage   wage

"It's like being on stage.
Let me out or pay me a wage!"
The monkey screeched in a rage
As it rattled the bars of its cage.

paint
rhyming sound -aint

complaint   faint   quaint   saint   taint

paste
rhyming sound -aste

haste   taste   waste

-aste rhymes with *-aced*
braced   disgraced   embraced   faced   graced   laced   paced
placed   raced   replaced   spaced   traced

Other words that rhyme with *paste*
chased   waist

pond
rhyming sound -ond

beyond   blond   bond   fond   respond

Another word that rhymes with *pond* is
wand

Said the frog in the pond,
"Please kiss me or wave your wand."
But the princess didn't respond.

pool
rhyming sound -ool

cool   drool   fool   school   spool   stool
toadstool   tool   whirlpool

-ool rhymes with *-ule*
capsule   globule   miniscule   molecule
mule   ridicule   rule   schedule   yule

Other words that rhyme with *pool*
fuel   ghoul

In our school
There's an empty stool
Where nobody sits
Except the ghoul
Of the pupil who died
While playing the fool.

post
rhyming sound -ost

almost   ghost   host   most
signpost   utmost

-ost rhymes with *-oast*
boast   coast
roast   toast

At the Halloween Ball
Our host was a ghost
Who walked through the wall.

pot
rhyming sound -ot

apricot blot cannot clot cot dot earshot forgot got
hot jackpot jot knot lot mascot not plot robot rot
Scot shot slot snot spot swot tot trot

Other words that rhyme with *pot*
squat swat what yacht

Ned Nott was shot
And Sam Shott was not.
So it's better to be Shott than Nott.

Anon

print
rhyming sound -int

flint footprint glint
hint lint mint
skint splint sprint
squint tint

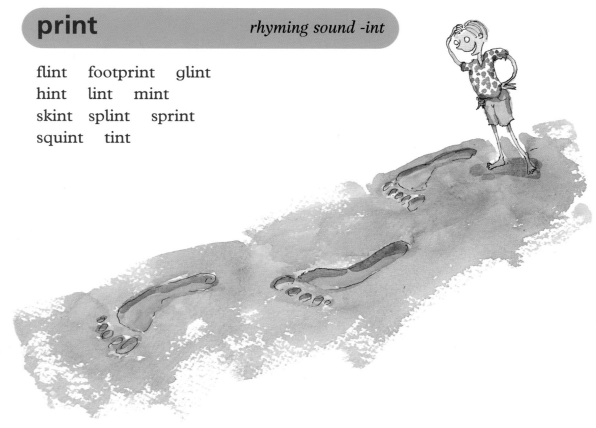

puff
rhyming sound -uff

bluff   buff   cuff   dandruff   duff   fluff   gruff   handcuff
huff   scruff   scuff   snuff   stuff

Some *-ough* words rhyme with *puff*
enough   rough   tough

pull
rhyming sound -ull

bull   full

-ull rhymes with *-ul*
armful   awful   beautiful   careful   cheerful   doubtful
dreadful   faithful   fearful   graceful   harmful   hopeful
joyful   playful   useful   wonderful

Another word that rhymes with *pull* is
wool

Qq

queen
rhyming sound -een

been   between   canteen   green   keen   preen   screen   seen
sheen   spleen   teen   thirteen   fourteen (etc)

-een rhymes with *-ean*
bean   clean   glean   Jean   lean   mean   wean

-een also rhymes with *-ine*
limousine   magazine   routine   sardine   tangerine   trampoline

-een also rhymes with *-ene*
gene   hygiene   scene   serene

"I'm a queen," said Kathleen.
"We've been filming a scene.
That's my picture in a magazine
And over there's my limousine."
"Dream on," said Jean.

quick
rhyming sound -ick

brick   chick   click   flick   gimmick   kick   lick   limerick
pick   prick   sick   slick   stick   thick   tick   trick   wick

-ick rhymes with *-ic*
attic   basic   comic   elastic   electric   fantastic   frantic
garlic   lunatic   magic   music   panic   picnic   plastic   public
supersonic   terrific   tragic

Rr

rain
rhyming sound -ain

again   brain   chain   complain   contain   drain   entertain
explain   gain   grain   main   obtain   pain   plain   refrain
remain   Spain   sprain   stain   strain   train   vain

-ain rhymes with *-ane*
cane   crane   Jane   lane   mane   pane   plane   sane   vane

Other words that rhyme with *rain*
rein   vein   reign

There was a young girl called Elaine
Who was dreadfully sick on the train –
Not once but again and again!

red
rhyming sound -ed

bed   bled   bred   fed   fled   led   moped   quadruped   red
shed   shred   sled   sped   Ted   wed

-ed words rhyme with some *-ead* words
ahead   bread   dead   dread   head   instead   lead   read
spread   thread   tread   widespread

Another word that rhymes with *red* is
said

"I sped down the hill on my sled,
But I crashed and demolished the shed,"
Said Ted, as he lay on the bed
Feeling the bump on his head.

ride

aside   astride   beside   bride   collide   countryside   decide
divide   glide   guide   hide   inside   pride   provide   side
slide   stride   tide   wide

-ide rhymes with *-ied*
cried   defied   denied   died   dried   fried   horrified   lied
spied   terrified   tied   tried

Other words that rhyme with *ride*
dyed   eyed   I'd   sighed

b
c
d
e
f
g
h
i
j
k
l
m
n
o
p
q
r
s
t
u
v
w
x
y
z

92

river

rhyming sound -iver

deliver   liver   quiver   shiver   sliver

It made me shake.
It made me shiver.
When the highwayman's ghost

Shouted,
"Stand and deliver!"

a b c d e f g h i j k l m n o p q r s t u v w x y z

road

rhyming sound -oad

goad   load   toad

-oad rhymes with *-ode*

code   episode   erode   explode   mode   ode   rode   strode

-oad also rhymes with *-owed*

burrowed   crowed   flowed   glowed   mowed   owed   rowed
showed   slowed   snowed   stowed   towed

Here lies the body of a toad.
Who forgot his Highway Code.
And didn't wait till the traffic slowed,
Before he tried to cross the road.

room
rhyming sound -oom

bloom   boom   bridegroom   broom   doom   gloom   groom
heirloom   loom   mushroom   zoom

-oom rhymes with *-ume*
costume   flume   fume   perfume   plume

Other words that rhyme with *room*
tomb   whom   womb

A skeleton once in Khartoum
Invited a ghost to his room
They spent the whole night
In the eeriest fight
As to who should be frightened of whom.

Anon

rope   *rhyming sound -ope*

antelope   cope   dope   elope   envelope   grope   hope
horoscope   lope   microscope   mope   pope   scope   slope
telescope   tightrope

Another word that rhymes with *rope* is
soap

**" I hope I can cope," said the antelope
as it started to walk along the tightrope.**

round   *rhyming sound -ound*

around   astound   background   bound
found   ground   hound   mound   pound
profound   sound   surround   wound

-ound rhymes with *-owned*
browned   clowned   crowned   downed   drowned
frowned   renowned

**My heart begins to pound
As I spin round and round,
On the whirling, twirling wheel
And I wish I was on the ground!**

rumble   *rhyming sound -umble*

bumble   crumble   fumble   grumble
humble   jumble   mumble   stumble   tumble

rush
rhyming sound -ush

blush brush crush flush gush hush lush mush
plush shush slush thrush

Ss

score
rhyming sound -ore

adore   ashore   before   bore   carnivore   chore   core   encore
explore   galore   gore   ignore   more   ore   pore   shore
snore   sore   store   swore   therefore   tore   wore

-ore rhymes with *-oar*
boar   oar   roar   soar

-ore also rhymes with *-aw*
caw   claw   draw   flaw   gnaw   guffaw   jackdaw
jaw   law   outlaw   paw   raw   saw   seesaw   straw   thaw

Other words that rhyme with *score*
corridor   dinosaur   door
drawer   floor   for   four
indoor   meteor   nor   or
outdoor   pour   war
your

shirt
rhyming sound -irt

dirt   flirt   skirt   squirt

-irt rhymes with *-urt*
blurt   curt   hurt   spurt

-irt also rhymes with *-ert*
advert   alert   Bert   concert   desert
dessert   expert   pert

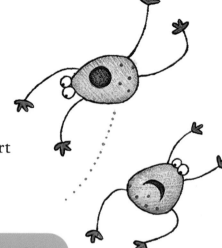

shop
rhyming sound -op

bop   chop   clop   cop   crop   drop   flip-flop   flop
hop   lollipop   lop   mop   plop   pop   prop   shop
slop   stop   top

Another word that rhymes
with *shop* is
swap

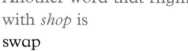

When the giant dived in the lake
There was an enormous plop,
And water flew up everywhere
'Cause he did a belly-flop.

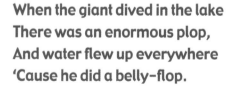

a
b
c
d
e
f
g
h
i
j
k
l
m
n
o
p
q
r
s
t
u
v
w
x
y
z

smile

rhyming sound -ile

agile   awhile   crocodile   file   fragile
hostile   mile   missile   mobile   pile   profile
reptile   stile   tile   vile   while

Other words that rhyme with *smile*
aisle   dial   I'll   isle   style   trial

"I'll dine in style," said the crocodile,
Giving a smile,
As he sharpened his teeth with a file.

snow

rhyming sound -ow

arrow   below   blow   bow   burrow   crow   elbow   flow
glow   grow   hedgerow   know   low   marrow   meadow   mow
pillow   rainbow   row   scarecrow   shadow   shallow   show
slow   sorrow   sow   stow   throw   tomorrow   tow   window

-ow rhymes with *-o*
ago   armadillo   buffalo   commando   disco   domino   echo
go   halo   hello   hero   hippo   logo   macho   mosquito   no
patio   photo   piano   potato   radio   rodeo   so   solo   stereo
studio   tornado   UFO   video   volcano   yo-yo   zero

-ow also rhymes with *-oe*
doe   foe   hoe   Joe   mistletoe   oboe   toe   woe

Other words that rhyme with *snow*
although   dough   owe   sew   though

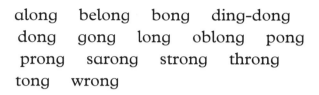

song
rhyming sound -ong

along   belong   bong   ding-dong
dong   gong   long   oblong   pong
prong   sarong   strong   throng
tong   wrong

spade
rhyming sound -ade

arcade   barricade   blade   decade   evade   fade
grade   invade   jade   lemonade   made
marmalade   parade   persuade   shade
trade   wade

-ade rhymes with *-aid*

afraid   aid   braid   laid   maid   mermaid   paid
raid   staid

-ade also rhymes with *-ayed*

arrayed   betrayed   decayed   delayed   frayed   played
prayed   sprayed   stayed   strayed   swayed   X-rayed

Other words that rhyme with *spade*
neighed   obeyed   preyed   suede   surveyed   weighed

Jade shook the bottle of lemonade,
Then she opened it and we all got sprayed.

a
b
c
d
e
f
g
h
i
j
k
l
m
n
o
p
q
r
s
t
u
v
w
x
y
z

speak
rhyming sound -eak

beak bleak creak freak leak peak sneak
squeak streak weak

-eak rhymes with *-eek*

cheek creek Greek leek meek peek reek seek
sleek week

-eak also rhymes with *-ique*

antique boutique clique technique unique

Another word that rhymes with *speak* is
shriek

**Two ghosts are playing hide-and-shriek.
They've been seeking each other since last week.**

sport
rhyming sound -ort

airport   export   fort   import   passport   port   report
resort   short   snort   sort   support   transport

Sean Short bought some shorts,
The shorts were shorter than
Sean Short thought.
Sean Short's short shorts were so short
Sean Short thought, "Sean you ought
Not to have bought shorts so short."

-ort rhymes with *-aught*
caught   distraught   fraught   onslaught   taught

-ort also rhymes with *-ought*
bought   brought   fought   nought   ought   sought
thought

-ort words rhyme with some *-art* words
quart   thwart   wart

Other words that rhyme with *sport*
astronaut   court   juggernaut   taut

stamp
rhyming sound -amp

amp   camp   champ   clamp   cramp
damp   lamp   ramp   scamp   tramp

storm
rhyming sound -orm

dorm   form   norm   perform   uniform

-orm words rhyme with some *-arm* words
swarm   warm

sun

rhyming sound -un

begun   bun   fun   gun   nun   pun   run   shun   spun   stun

-un words also rhyme with some *-one* words
done   none   one   someone

-un words also rhyme with some *-on* words
son   ton   won

A rabbit raced a turtle.
The turtle easily won.
The rabbit came in second,
A little hot cross bun.

Anon

swim

rhyming sound -im

brim   dim   grim   him   Jim   Kim   prim   rim   skim   slim
Tim   trim   whim

Other words that rhyme with *swim*
gym   hymn   limb   pseudonym   synonym

a b c d e f g h i j k l m n o p q r s t u v w x y z

105

Tt

table — *rhyming sound -able*

able cable fable stable timetable

Another word that rhymes with *table* is
label

tail — *rhyming sound -ail*

ail bail detail fail frail hail jail mail nail pail
quail rail sail snail trail wail

-ail rhymes with *-ale*
ale bale dale exhale female gale impale inhale
male nightingale pale sale scale stale tale telltale
whale

A whale in a veil getting married in a gale.

Another word that rhymes with *tail* is
veil

talk
rhyming sound -alk

chalk   stalk   walk

-alk rhymes with *-ork*
cork   fork   pork   stork

-alk also rhymes with *-awk*
gawk   hawk   squawk   tomahawk

a
b
c
d
e
f
g
h
i
j
k
l
m
n
o
p
q
r
s
t
u
v
w
x
y
z

107

tent

rhyming sound -ent

accident   ascent   bent   cement   cent   compliment   consent
content   dent   descent   dissent   event   experiment   fragment
frequent   invent   lent   ornament   present   prevent   recent
relent   rent   resent   scent   sent   spent   torment   vent
went

Other words that rhyme with *tent*
leant   meant

We could not get rid of the scent
That a cow had left outside the tent!

tickle

rhyming sound -ickle

fickle   pickle   prickle   sickle   trickle

Another word that rhymes with *tickle* is
icicle

Don't tickle a thistle or you'll get in a pickle,
For thistles are prickly and thistles'll prickle.

tie

rhyming sound -ie

die   lie   pie   untie

-ie rhymes with *-y*

ally   butterfly   by   cry   deny   dry   fly   fry   horrify
July   layby   lullaby   magnify   multiply   my   mystify
nearby   petrify   pigsty   pry   rely   reply   satisfy   shy   sky
sly   spy   sty   supply   terrify   try   why   wry

-ie also rhymes with *-igh*

high   sigh   thigh

Other words that rhyme with *tie*

alibi   buy   bye   dye   eye   goodbye   I   guy

Georgie Porgie shouted "Hi!"
To a girl as she passed by.
"Give me a kiss. Don't be shy."
"Give you a kiss! I'd rather die."

time
rhyming sound -ime

chime crime grime lime mime pantomine
prime slime

Other words that rhyme with *time*
climb enzyme I'm rhyme thyme

tower
rhyming sound -ower

cauliflower cower flower glower power shower

Some *-our* words rhyme with *tower*
devour flour hour our scour sour

town
rhyming sound -own

brown   clown   crown   down   drown   frown   gown

Another word that rhymes with *town* is
noun

toy
rhyming sound -oy

ahoy   alloy   annoy   boy   buoy   convoy   corduroy
cowboy   coy   destroy   employ   enjoy   joy   ploy   Roy

tree
rhyming sound -ee

agree   bee   chimpanzee   coffee   degree   disagree   fee
flee   free   glee   guarantee   jamboree   jubilee   knee
marquee   pedigree   referee   refugee   see   settee   spree
tee   three   toffee   wee

-ee rhymes with *-ea*
flea   pea   plea   sea   tea

Other words that rhyme with *tree*
be   chimney   donkey   genie   grafitti
he   honey   key   macaroni   me   money
monkey   pixie   quay   recipe   she   ski
valley   we

trunk

rhyming sound -unk

bunk   chipmunk   chunk   clunk   drunk   dunk   hunk   junk
punk   shrunk   skunk   slunk   stunk   sunk

Another word that rhymes with *trunk* is
monk

**"After the skunk slunk over my bunk,
it stunk!" said the monk.**

a
b
c
d
e
f
g
h
i
j
k
l
m
n
o
p
q
r
s
t
u
v
w
x
y
z

113

Uu

under
rhyming sound -under

blunder   plunder   thunder

Another word that rhymes with *under* is wonder

The pirates made a dreadful blunder
By trying to hide all their plunder
Beneath a tree during the thunder.
Now they're lying six feet under!

up
rhyming sound -up

buttercup   cup   hiccup   pickup   pup   sup

loot

114

urn

rhyming sound -urn

burn   churn   return   spurn   turn

-urn rhymes with *-earn*
earn   learn   yearn

-urn also rhymes with *-ern*
concern   fern   stern

us

rhyming sound -us

bonus   bus   cactus   circus   crocus   genius   hippopotamus
minus   octopus   plus   pus   radius   thus   virus   walrus

-us rhymes with *-uss*
discuss   fuss

-us also rhymes with *-ous*
anxious   callous   courageous   curious   dubious   enormous
envious   fabulous   famous   furious   glorious   gorgeous
hideous   hilarious   horrendous   ingenious   jealous   ludicrous
marvellous   mischievous   monstrous   mysterious   nervous
obvious   precious   raucous   ravenous   serious
tremendous   various   wondrous

The driver caused an awful fuss
When we tried to board the bus
With our hippopotamus.

a
b
c
d
e
f
g
h
i
j
k
l
m
n
o
p
q
r
s
t
u
v
w
x
y
z

use

rhyming sound -use

abuse   accuse   amuse   confuse   enthuse   excuse   fuse
muse   refuse   ruse

-use also rhymes with *-ews*
chews   news   screws   stews

-use also rhymes with *-ues*
blues   clues   hues   queues

-use also rhymes with *-ooze*
booze   ooze   snooze

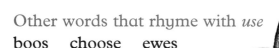

Other words that rhyme with *use*
boos   choose   ewes
kangaroos   lose
tattoos   views   whose   zoos

**Gnus who choose to read the news
Share their views in queues in zoos.**

Vv

van

rhyming sound -an

an ban began bran can caravan catamaran clan
deadpan fan flan gran Japan man marzipan nan
orang-utan pan plan ran scan span Stan tan than

A young man who came from Japan
Taught his orang-utan to cancan.
When I asked if he can,
The young man from Japan
Said, "Can he cancan? Yes, he can!"

117

vest

rhyming sound -est

arrest   bequest   best   chest   conquest   contest
crest   detest   digest   guest   infest   invest   jest
lest   nest   pest   protest   quest   request   rest
suggest   test   west   zest

-est rhymes with *-essed*

addressed   blessed   caressed
confessed   depressed   digressed
distressed   dressed   expressed
guessed   impressed
messed   obsessed
possessed
pressed
progressed
stressed

Ww

wall
rhyming sound -all

all ball call fall football hall mall pall small
squall stall tall

-all rhymes with *-awl*
bawl brawl crawl drawl
scrawl shawl sprawl
trawl

-all also rhymes with *-aul*
caterwaul haul maul
Paul

There was a young fellow called Paul
Who went to a fancy dress ball.
But he made a mistake
'Cause he went as a cake
And a dog ate him up in the hall.

weed

rhyming sound -eed

agreed   bleed   breed   creed   deed   exceed   freed
greed   guaranteed   heed   indeed   need   proceed
reed   refereed   seed   speed   steed   succeed   tweed

-eed words rhyme with some *-ead* words
bead   knead   lead   plead   read

-eed words rhyme with some *-ede* words
centipede   concede   millipede   stampede   swede

well

rhyming sound -ell

bell   cell   dwell   farewell   fell   hell   quell   sell
shell   smell   spell   swell   tell   unwell   yell

Other words that rhyme with *well*
caramel   carousel   excel   gel   hotel
lapel   motel   parallel
propel   rebel

Spinning round on the carousel
Sound the horn and ring the bell.
Feel the fairground's magic spell
Spinning round on the carousel.

wheel

rhyming sound -eel

eel feel heel keel kneel peel reel steel

-eel rhymes with *-eal*

appeal conceal deal heal ideal meal ordeal peal real reveal seal squeal steal veal zeal

win

rhyming sound -in

begin bin cabin chin coffin din dolphin fin goblin gremlin grin in javelin kin margin muffin origin penguin pin puffin pumpkin robin ruin satin sequin shin sin skin spin thin tin twin violin vitamin within

Other words that rhyme with *win*

examine inn

**When Violet plays her violin
She makes a really awful din.
I'm glad she hasn't got a twin!**

wise

rhyming sound -ise

advertise   advise   apologise   arise   clockwise   disguise
exercise   guise   likewise   organise   prise   revise   rise
sunrise   surprise

-ise rhymes with *-ies*

cries   dies   dries   flies   fries   horrifies   lies   lullabies
petrifies   pies   replies   skies   spies   terrifies   ties   tries

-ise also rhymes with *-ize*

capsize   hypnotize   idolise   prize
realize   recognize   size

Other words that rhyme with *wise*

buys   eyes   highs   sighs   thighs

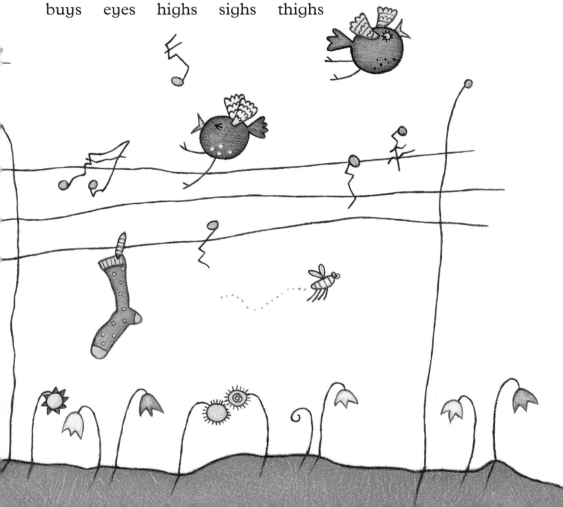

a
b
c
d
e
f
g
h
i
j
k
l
m
n
o
p
q
r
s
t
u
v
w
x
y
z

Xx

X-ray

rhyming sound -ay

alleyway anyway away bay betray birthday bray clay day decay delay display essay fray hay holiday hooray hurray lay may midday Monday (etc) motorway OK pay pray railway ray say spray stay stowaway straightaway subway sway takeaway today tray way yesterday

-ay rhymes with *-eigh*
neigh sleigh weigh

-ay also rhymes with *-ey*
disobey grey hey obey prey survey they

Other words that rhyme with *X-ray*
ballet bret bouquet buffet cafe chalet croquet duvet fiancé(e) paté ricochet sachet

When Auntie Fay began to neigh
And spend the day just eating hay,
My uncle said, "I cannot say
Why she's behaving in this way.
I'd better put her in the stable
In the stall next to your Auntie Mabel."

a
b
c
d
e
f
g
h
i
j
k
l
m
n
o
p
q
r
s
t
u
v
w
x
y
z

125

Yy

yard

rhyming sound -ard

bard bombard card discard hard
lard leotard postcard regard shard

-ard rhymes with *-arred*
barred charred jarred marred
scarred sparred starred tarred

Another word that rhymes with *yard* is
guard

126

yellow
rhyming sound -ellow

bellow   fellow   mellow

Other words that rhyme with *yellow*
cello   hello

I was practising playing the cello,
When I heard someone give a loud bellow,
"For goodness sake
You make my ears ache.
Please stop it. There's a good fellow!"

127

Zz

zip
rhyming sound -ip

blip championship chip clip dip drip equip fingertip
flip friendship gossip grip hardship hip kip leadership
lip microchip nip paperclip pip quip rip ship sip
skip slip snip strip tip trip tulip whip

zoo
rhyming sound -oo

a-choo bamboo boo coo cuckoo hullaballoo igloo
kangaroo loo moo shampoo shoo tattoo too voodoo
woo yoo-hoo

-oo rhymes with *-ew*
askew blew brew chew corkscrew crew dew drew
few flew grew interview knew mew nephew new
pew phew screw shrew sinew skew slew threw view

-oo also rhymes with *-ue*
argue avenue barbecue blue clue continue cue due
flue fondue glue hue queue revue rue statue subdue
sue tissue true value venue

Other words that rhyme with *zoo*
canoe   do   ewe   flu   gnu   guru
Hindu   kungfu   menu   Peru
rendezvous   shoe   tai-kwando
through   to   tutu
two   you

There was an old man from Peru
Who dreamed he was eating his shoe
He woke in the night
In a terrible fright
And found it was perfectly true.

Anon

a
b
c
d
e
f
g
h
i
j
k
l
m
n
o
p
q
r
s
t
u
v
w
x
y
z

Write your own poetry

Limericks

A limerick is a five line verse which follows a set pattern. It was first made famous by the poet Edward Lear (1812-88). You can find examples of limericks on pages 58 (**There was once a boy called Bill**), 117 (**A young man who came from Japan**) and 129 (**There was an old man from Peru**).

In a limerick
- ▸ lines 1 and 2 are longer lines that end with a rhyme
- ▸ lines 3 and 4 are shorter lines that end with a rhyme
- ▸ line 5 is a longer line that rhymes with lines 1 and 2

Can you complete these limericks?

> **There was a young schoolboy called Flynn**
> **Who sat on a drawing pin**
> **He leapt up in the air...**

You can find words with the rhyming sound -*in* listed under the entry for **win** on page 122 and words with the rhyming sound -*air* under the entry for **air** on page 8.

> **A daring young girl from Dundee...**

You can find words with the rhyming sound -*ee* listed under the entry for **tree** on page 112.

> **A wizard's apprentice called Matt...**

You can find words with the rhyming sound -*at* listed under the entry for **hat** on page 49.

Now see if you can make up a limerick on your own. Try to think of a funny punchline to end it.

Nonsense nursery rhymes

Nonsense nursery rhymes are modern versions of traditional nursery rhymes. For example:

> Mary had a little cow.
> She fed it safety pins
> And every time she milked the cow
> The milk came out in tins.

Here are the first lines of some nonsense nursery rhymes. Can you complete them?

▸ **Mary had a little cat.**
  She dressed it in a skirt...

▸ **Little Miss Kettle**
  Sat on a nettle...

▸ **Humpty Dumpty sat on the sofa**
  Watching cartoons on TV.

▸ **Billy, my brother and I fell out**
  And what do you think it was all about?

▸ **Little Tom Tarpet sat on the carpet**
  Licking a big ice cream...

▸ **Dr Lester went to Chester...**

▸ **Little Bo-Peep can't get to sleep...**

▸ **Monday's child has a goofy grin...**

Counting rhymes

A counting rhyme is a rhyme which includes counting.
Some rhymes count up to ten, others count backwards from 10
down to 1.

Can you complete these counting rhymes?

One, two

One, two
A bath full of glue

Three, four....

Ten Naughty Dragons

Ten naughty dragons blowing smoke-rings in a line,
One set himself on fire then there were nine.

Nine naughty dragons....

Animal Counting Rhyme

One for the goat in a winter coat.
Two for the ants in striped underpants,
Three for the...

Ten Young Children

Ten young children
 Playing in the park.
The first one said,
 "Pretend I'm a shark."
The second one said,
 "I'm a dinosaur."
The third one said...

Rhyming riddles

The poems on this page are rhyming riddles. Can you solve them?

1

I can spin. I can roll. I can fly through the air.
I go where you hit me. Then I lie waiting there.
   I am usually round – sometimes big, sometimes small.
    I can make my way over or back from a wall.

2

   My first is in ghoul and also in charm.
   My second is in magic and twice in alarm.
 My third is in cauldron but isn't in fire.
My fourth is in gremlin but not in vampire.
My fifth is in skeleton and in bones.
My sixth is in werewolf but isn't in groans.
My seventh is in spell but not in broomstick.
My eighth's found in treat, but not found in trick.
My ninth is in phantom but isn't in fear.
My whole is the scariest night of the year.

3

Hold it steady in your hand,
Then you will see another land,
Where right is left, and left is right,
And no sound stirs by day or night;
When you look in, yourself you'll see,
Yet in that place you cannot be.

Here is a riddle about an animal with the rhyming words missing. Can you work out what the words are and what the animal is?

> I scratch the leaves that have fallen ____
> I am hard to see as my spines are ____
> I use the strong claws upon my ___
> To search for insects and slugs to ___.
> Soon I'll curl in a ball in my ____
> And go to sleep for my winter ____

Make up a rhyming riddle of you own. Either choose a subject yourself or write a riddle about an animal or an object, such as a pen, a book or a bicycle.

Epitaphs

An epitaph is a verse written about a person or animal who has died. It is often put on their gravestone. Here are some examples:

> Here lies the body
> Of Percy Thistle
> A ref who's blown
> His final whistle.
>
> Here lies a teacher Mr Lee
> Who said, "You'll be the death of me"!
> And sitting at his desk one day
> He gave a sigh and passed away.
>
> In loving memory of Rover
> Who ran out in the road
> And got run over.

Answers: down brown feet eat nest rest (a hedgehog)

In memory of Charlotte Cul-de-sac,
A loyal and trusted friend
Who finally lived up to her name
And came to a dead end.

Can you complete these epitaphs?

▸ Here lie the remains of Auntie Vi
  Who strapped on wings and tried to fly...

▸ In memory of Billy Green
  Who took off in a time machine...

▸ Here lies what's left of Mr Bloor...

▸ Here lies a careless boy called Jake...

▸ In memory of fearless Fred...

▸ In memory of little Red Riding Hood...

Can you write some epitaphs of your own?

You could write about a person or an animal – either real or imaginary. For example, you could write about a nursery rhyme character, such as Old King Cole, an imaginary creature, such as Desmond Dinosaur, or a person with an unusual name, such as Candy Bar.

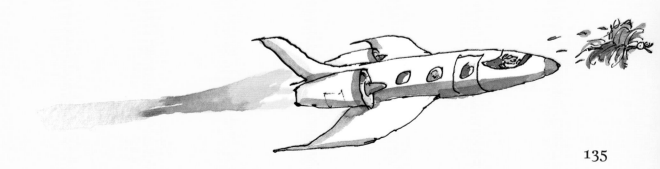

Rapping

Rapping is a popular type of rhyming poetry. A rap is a poem with plenty of rhyming and a very strong rhythm, which is often written to be performed.

Can you add some verses to this rap about people and their names?

Clap your hands, tap your feet,
Get the rhythm, get the beat.

My name's Grace. I am just ace.
I have got a smile on my face.

Clap your hands, tap your feet,
Get the rhythm, get the beat.

My name's Nasreen. I'm lean and mean.
I'm a star of the disco scene.

Clap your hands, tap your feet,
Get the rhythm, get the beat...

Can you write a fairground rap?
Here are two lines that you can use to get started:

C'mon everybody, let's go to the fair,
There's plenty of things for us to do there...

You can write a rap about any topic.
Choose your own subject and write a rap about it.
You could use these two lines to start your rap:

Come on everybody, let's hear you clap
We're going to do the ... rap.

Rhyming couplets

One of the ways poets use rhymes is to write rhyming couplets.
A rhyming couplet is a pair of lines that rhyme.

Example:

> We like riding on the double-decker bus,
> Up on the top-deck, that's the place for us!

Can you add some rhyming couplets to this list poem?

In my magic box

> In my magic box, I will put
>
> The twang of a guitar
> The silver lining of a star
>
> The juicy ripeness of a peach
> The sunlight shining on a beach...

Here is cautionary rhyme, written in couplets:

Warning: Too Much TV Can Damage Your Health

> This is the tale of Millie Mee
> Who day and night would watch TV.
> Now both her eyeballs have turned square,
> An aerial's growing in her hair.
> All she can do is watch TV
> For Millie's glued to the settee.
> So switch off now. Don't hesitate.
> Make sure you don't share Millie's fate.

Can you write some more couplets to complete these cautionary rhymes?

This is the tale of Samuel Sprocket
Who set off in his homemade rocket...

This is the tale of Betty Blair
Who never ever washed her hair...

A cheeky boy called Robert Rung
Was always sticking out his tongue..

Write a cautionary tale of your own, for example about someone who is always picking his nose or who is always boasting or about someone who does something silly. Write it in rhyming couplets.

Chants

Many chants, like this traditional one, are written in rhyming couplets:

Sam, Sam, the Dirty Old Man

Sam, Sam, the dirty old man,
Washed his face in a frying pan.
He combed his hair with a donkey's tail
And scratched his belly with his big toenail.

Teacher, Teacher

Teacher, teacher, please come quick
Jennifer Brown's been terribly sick.

Can you complete these 'Teacher, teacher' chants?

Teacher, teacher, what should I do?...

Teacher, teacher, come and have a look...

138

Teacher, teacher, look over there...

Teacher, teacher, help me please...

I Know a Man...

I know a man who wears smelly socks.
I know a man who thinks he's a fox.

Can you complete these 'I know a man' chants?

I know a man with toes on his head...

I know a man whose nose is square...

I know a man who lives in a drain...

I know a man who's the size of a flea...

Homophones

A homophone is one of a group of words which sound the same but have a different meaning or spelling. For example, hare and hair are homophones.

Can you find the homophones in these rhymes?

Bare Bear hasn't any hair.
That's why Bare Bear is bare.

Nobody asked her to dance at all,
So she had a good bawl at the ball.

"No, I don't know what to do,"
I said to the man in the queue.
"So I'll take my cue from you."

A gnu who was new to the zoo
Asked another gnu what he should do.
The other gnu said,
Shaking his head,
"If I knew, I'd tell you, I'm new too!"

Rose grows rows of roses.
Each rose Rose grows grows in a row.

Now use this dictionary to find homophones for these words:

beach   board   great   need   pale   pane
pear   read   right   road   sell   sew   sore   stair

Which of the above words has more than one other homophone?

Rhyme patterns

Many poems have four-line verses. A four-line verse is called a quatrain.
Quatrains can have a number of different rhyming patterns.

Pattern 1

In this verse the first and second lines rhyme and the third and fourth
lines rhyme.

   As I was going out one day
   My head fell off and rolled away.
   But when I saw that it was gone,
   I picked it up and put it on.

Can you complete the second verse of the poem?

   And when I got into the ....
   A fellow cried, "Look at your ....!"
   I looked at them and sadly .....
   "I've left them both asleep in ....!"

140

Pattern 2

This poem has verses in which the second line rhymes with the fourth line.

> We are the gremlins.
>   We're up to no good.
>   We do things we shouldn't,
>   Not things that we should.
>
>   We get up to mischief
>   Of every sort.
>   But we're cunning and clever,
>   We never get caught.

Can you complete the next verse of the poem?

> We are the gremlins.
> We disconnect wires...

Can you add some more verses in the same pattern describing other things that the gremlins do?

Pattern 3

In this verse the first line rhymes with the third line and the second line rhymes with the fourth line.

> When the night is as cold as stone,
> When lightning severs the sky,
> When your blood is chilled to the bone,
> That's the hour when the witches fly.

Can you complete this verse about a mad magician using the same rhyme pattern?

> In his dark cave the mad magician dwells...

Pattern 4

Sometimes poets write lines in which there is a rhyme within the line. For example:

When Aunty Joan became a phone...

This is known as internal rhyme.

In the following verse the second line rhymes with the fourth line and there are internal rhymes in the first and third lines:

Elastic Jones had rubber bones.
He could bounce up and down like a ball.
When he was six, one of his tricks
Was jumping a ten-foot wall.

Can you complete this verse using the same rhyme pattern:

Ferdinand Fry boasted, "I can fly!"...

Now try to write a poem about a pirate called Peg-Leg Poll in four-line verses, using one of these rhyming patterns.

Index of rhyming sounds

-ab see **crab**

-able see **table**

-ace see **face**

-aced see **paste**

-ack see **back**

-acked see **act**

-act see **act**

-ad see **dad**

-ade see **spade**

-ag see **flag**

-age see **page**

-aid see **spade**

-aight see **gate**

-ail see **tail**

-aim see **name**

-ain see **rain**

-aint see **paint**

-air see **air**

-aire see **air**

-airy see **hairy**

-aist see **paste**

-ait see **gate**

-ake see **lake**

-ale see **tail**

-alk see **talk**

-all see **wall**

-alm see **arm**

-am see **jam**

-ame see **name**

-amp see **stamp**

-an see **van**

-ance see **dance**

-and see **hand**

-ane see **rain**

-ang see **bang**

-ank see **bank**

-anned see **hand**

-ant see **ant**

-ap see **map**

-ape see **grape**

-ar see **car**

-ard see **yard**

-are see **air**

-ark see **dark**

-arm (as in harm) see **arm**

-arm (as in warm) see **storm**

-arred see **yard**

-art (as in start) see **cart**

-art (as in wart) see **sport**

-ary see **hairy**

-ase see **face**

-ash see **crash**

-ask see **ask**

-ass see **glass**

-ast see **last**

-aste see **paste**

-at see **hat**

-atch see **catch**

-ate see **gate**

-aught see **sport**

-aul see **wall**

-ave see **cave**

-aw see **score**

-awk see **talk**

-awl see **wall**

-awn see **corn**

-ay see **X-ray**

-ayed see **spade**

-ayer see **air**

-ea see **tree**

-each see **beach**

-ead (as in head) see **red**

-ead (as in bead) see **weed**

-eak (as in beak) see **speak**

-eak (as in break) see **cake**

-eal see **wheel**

-eam see **dream**

-ean see **queen**

-eap see **keep**

-ear (as in fear) see **ear**

-ear (as in bear) see **air**

-earn see **urn**

-eas see **freeze**

-ease see **freeze**

-east see **east**

-eat (as in heat) see **meat**

-eat (as in sweat) see **jet**

-eck see **neck**

-ed see **red**

-ede see **weed**

-ee see **tree**

-eech see **beach**

-eed see **weed**

-eek see **speak**

-eel see **wheel**

-eem see **dream**

-een see **queen**

-eep see **keep**

-eer see **ear**

-ees see **freeze**

-eet see **meat**

-eeze see **freeze**

-eg see **leg**

-eigh see **X-ray**

-el see **well**

-elf see **elf**

-ell see **well**

-ellow see **yellow**

-elt see **belt**

-en see **hen**

-end see **end**

-ene see **queen**

-ent see **tent**

-ept see **crept**

-er (as in her) see **fur**

-erd see **bird**

-ere (as in here) see **ear**

-ere (as in where) see **air**

-ere (as in were) see **fur**

-ern see **urn**

-erry see **merry**

-ert see **shirt**

-ess see **dress**

-essed see **vest**

-est see **vest**

-et see **jet**

-ete see **meat**

-ette see **jet**

-ettle see **nettle**

-ever see **ever**

-ew (as in chew)
see **zoo**

-ew (as in sew)
see **snow**

-ewed see **food**

-ewn (as in sewn)
see **bone**

-ews (as in sews)
see **nose**

-ews (as in news)
see **use**

-ey (as in key)
see **tree**

-ey (as in they)
see **X-ray**

-ic see **quick**

-ice (as in ice)
see **ice**

-ice (as in practice)
see **kiss**

-ich see **itch**

-ick see **quick**

-ickle see **tickle**

-icks see **mix**

-ics see **mix**

-id see **lid**

-iddle see **middle**

-ide see **ride**

-idge see **bridge**

-ie see **tie**

-ied see **ride**

-ier see **ear**

-ies see **wise**

-iews (as in views)
see **use**

-ig see **big**

-igh see **tie**

-ighs see **wise**

-ight see **light**

-ign see **nine**

-ike see **bike**

-il see **ill**

-ile see **smile**

-ill see **ill**

-im see **swim**

-ime see **time**

-imp see **imp**

-in see **win**

-ind see **find**

-ine (as in
magazine)
see **queen**

-ine (as in fine)
see **nine**

-ing see **king**

-ink see **ink**

-inner see **dinner**

-int see **print**

-ip see **zip**

-ique see **speak**

-ir see **fur**

-ird see **bird**

-ire see **fire**

-irl see **girl**

-irr see **fur**

-irst see **first**

-irt see **shirt**

-ise (as in rise)
see **wise**

-ise (as in promise)
see **kiss**

-ise (as in paradise)
see **ice**

-ish see **fish**

-iss see **kiss**

-issed see **mist**

-ist see **mist**

-it see **hit**

-itch see **itch**

-ite see **light**

-ive see **five**

-iver see **river**

-ix see **mix**

-ize see **wise**

-o (as in slow)
see **snow**

-oad see **road**

-oak see **oak**

-oal see **hole**

-oap see **rope**

-oar see **score**

-oard see **lord**

-oast see **post**

-oat see **coat**

-ob see **job**

-ock see **knock**

-ocks see **fox**

-ode see **road**

-oe see **snow**

-oes see **nose**

-og see **dog**

-ogue see **dog**

-oil see **oil**

-oke see **oak**

-old see **old**

-ole see **hole**

-oll see **hole**

-ome (as in come)
see **mum**

-on (as in son)
see **sun**

-ond see **pond**

-onder see **under**

-one (as in phone)
see **bone**

-one (as in one)
see **sun**

-oney see **honey**

-ong see **song**

-oo see **zoo**

-ood (as in food)
see **food**

-ood (as in blood)
see **mud**

-ood (as in wood)
see **hood**

-ooed see **food**

-ook see **cook**

-ool see **pool**

-ool (as in wool)
see **pull**

-oom see **room**

-oon see **moon**

-oop see **hoop**

-oot see **boot**

-oor see **score**

-ooze see **use**

-op see **shop**

-ope see **rope**

-or see **score**

-ord see **lord**

-ore see **score**

-ored see **lord**

-ork see **talk**

-orm see **storm**

-orn see **corn**

-ort see **sport**

-os (as in radios) see **nose**

-ose see **nose**

-oss see **boss**

-ost see **post**

-ot see **pot**

-ote see **coat**

-other see **brother**

-ouble see **bubble**

-ough (as in rough) see **puff**

-ough (as in plough) see **cow**

-ought see **sport**

-ould see **hood**

-ounce see **bounce**

-ound see **round**

-oup see **hoop**

-our (as in pour) see **score**

-our (as in hour) see **tower**

-ous see **us**

-ouse see **house**

-out see **out**

-ove see **love**

-ow (as in now) see **cow**

-ow (as in blow) see **snow**

-owed see **road**

-owel see **owl**

-ower see **tower**

-owl see **owl**

-own see **town**

-own (as in phone, groan) see **bone**

-owned (as in crowned) see **round**

-ows see **nose**

-ox see **fox**

-oy see **toy**

-oyal see **oil**

-oze see **nose**

-ub see **grub**

-ubble see **bubble**

-uck see **duck**

-ud see **mud**

-ude see **food**

-ue see **zoo**

-ued see **food**

-ues (as in clues) see **use**

-uff see **puff**

-ug see **jug**

-ul see **pull**

-ule see **pool**

-ull see **pull**

-um see **mum**

-umb see **mum**

-umble see **rumble**

-ume see **room**

-ump see **jump**

-un see **sun**

-unch see **lunch**

-under see **under**

-une see **moon**

-ung see **lung**

-unk see **trunk**

-unny see **honey**

-unt see **hunt**

-up see **up**

-ur see **fur**

-url see **girl**

-urn see **urn**

-urr see **fur**

-urt see **shirt**

-us see **us**

-use see **use**

-ush see **rush**

-uss see **us**

-ust see **dust**

-ut see **hut**

-ute see **boot**

-uy see **tie**

-y see **tie**

-ye see **tie**

-yme see **time**

Alphabetical index

cardboard 69
care 8
career 32
careful 88
caressed 118
carnivore 98
carousel 120
carpet 60
cart 19
cartoon 75
case 34
cash 24
cashier 32
cask 10
casserole 50
cassette 60
cast 66
cat 49
catalogue 29
catamaran 117
catch 19
caterwaul 119
caught 103
cauliflower 111
cavalier 32
cave 20
caviar 18
caw 98
ceased 33
ceiling 64
celebrate 45
cell 120
cello 127
celt 12
cement 108
cent 108
centipede 120
chain 90

chair 8
chalet 124
chalk 107
champ 104
champi-
onship 128
chance 27
chap 71
charm 10
charred 126
chart 19
chase 34
chased 85
chat 49
cheap 63
cheat 72
check 78
cheek 102
cheep 63
cheer 32
cheerful 88
cheese 42
cheque 78
cherry 73
chess 30
chest 118
chestnut 55
chew 128
chewed 40
chews 116
chick 89
chicks 74
childhood 54
chill 58
chime 111
chimney 112
chimneys 42
chimp 59
chimpanzee 112
chimpanzees 42
chin 122

chink 59
chip 128
chipmunk 113
choir 38
choke 81
choose 116
chop 99
chord 69
chore 98
chose 80
chuck 30
chug 61
chum 75
chunk 113
churn 115
chute 15
cigar 18
circuit 49
circus 115
clad 27
claim 76
clamp 104
clan 117
clang 10
clank 11
clap 71
clarinet 60
clash 24
class 46
classed 66
claw 98
clay 124
clean 89
clear 32
clever 33
click 89
clicks 74
climb 111
cling 64
clink 59
clip 128
clique 102

cloak 81
clock 65
clocks 41
clockwise 123
clog 29
clone 14
clop 99
close 80
clot 87
clout 83
clown 112
clowned 96
club 47
cluck 30
clue 128
clues 116
clump 61
clung 70
clunk 113
coal 50
coast 86
coat 20
cob 61
code 94
coffee 112
coffin 122
coil 81
coke 81
cold 82
collide 92
combat 49
combine 79
come 75
comic 89
commando 100
common-
place 34
compact 8
compare 8
compete 72
complain 90

complaint 85
complete 72
compliment 108
conceal 122
concede 120
concentrate 45
concern 115
concert 99
concrete 72
cone 14
confess 30
confessed 118
confiscate 45
confuse 116
conquest 118
consent 108
console 50
consoled 82
contact 8
contain 90
content 108
contest 118
continue 128
contract 8
contrary 48
contrast 66
control 50
controlled 82
convoy 112
coo 128
cooed 40
cook 21
cool 86
coop 54
cop 99
cope 96
cord 69

corduroy 112
core 98
cork 107
corkscrew 128
corn 22
corridor 98
costume 95
cot 87
could 54
countryside 92
courageous 115
courgette 60
court 103
cow 23
cowboy 112
cower 111
cox 41
coy 112
crab 23
crack 13
cracked 8
crag 39
cram 60
cramp 104
crane 90
crank 11
crash 24
crate 45
crave 20
crawl 119
creak 102
cream 29
creased 33
create 45
creed 120
creek 102
creep 63
crept 26
cress 30

duvet *124*
dwell *120*
dwelt *12*
dye *110*
dyed *92*
dynamite *68*

E
each *11*
ear *32*
earl *46*
earn *115*
earshot *87*
earwig *12*
ease *42*
east *33*
eat *72*
echo *100*
educate *45*
eel *122*
egg *67*
eight *45*
elastic *89*
elbow *100*
elbows *80*
electric *89*
elegant *10*
elephant *10*
elf *33*
elope *96*
embark *28*
embrace *34*
embraced *85*
empire *38*
employ *112*
encore *98*
end *33*
engage *84*
engineer *32*
enjoy *112*
enormous *115*
enough *88*

enrage *84*
entertain *90*
enthuse *116*
entrance *27*
envelope *96*
envious *115*
enzyme *111*
episode *94*
equip *128*
erode *94*
escape *46*
essay *124*
estate *45*
estimate *45*
evade *101*
event *108*
ever *33*
ewe *129*
ewes *116*
exact *8*
exaggerate *45*
exam *60*
examine *122*
exceed *120*
excel *120*
except *26*
excess *30*
excite *68*
exclaim *76*
exclude *40*
excuse *116*
execute *15*
exercise *123*
exhale *106*
exit *49*
expand *48*
experiment *108*
expert *99*
explain *90*
explode *94*
explore *98*

explored *69*
export *103*
expose *80*
express *30*
expressed *118*
extend *33*
extract *8*
extreme *29*
eye *110*
eyebrow *23*
eyed *92*
eyes *123*

F
fab *23*
fable *106*
fabulous *115*
face *34*
faced *85*
fact *8*
fad *27*
fade *101*
fail *106*
faint *85*
fair *8*
fairy *48*
faithful *88*
fake *66*
fall *119*
falsehood *54*
fame *76*
famous *115*
fan *117*
fang *10*
fanned *48*
fantastic *89*
far *18*
fare *8*
farewell *120*
farm *10*
fascinate *45*
fast *66*

fat *49*
fate *45*
fawn *22*
fear *32*
fearful *88*
feast *33*
feat *72*
fed *91*
fee *112*
feed *120*
feel *122*
fees *42*
feet *72*
fell *120*
fellow *127*
felt *12*
female *106*
fen *49*
fern *115*
ferry *73*
fete *45*
fettle *78*
few *128*
fiancé(e) *124*
fickle *109*
fiddle *73*
fidget *60*
fig *12*
fight *68*
file *100*
fill *58*
fin *122*
find *36*
fine *79*
fined *36*
fingertip *128*
fir *44*
fire *38*
fireplace *34*
first *39*
fish *39*
fist *74*

fit *49*
five *39*
fix *74*
flab *23*
flag *39*
flair *8*
flake *66*
flame *76*
flan *117*
flap *71*
flapjack *13*
flash *24*
flask *10*
flat *49*
flaw *98*
flea *112*
fleas *42*
fleck *78*
fled *91*
flee *112*
flees *42*
fleet *72*
flew *128*
flick *89*
flicks *74*
flies *123*
fling *64*
flint *87*
flip *128*
flip-flop *99*
flirt *99*
flit *49*
float *20*
flock *65*
flocks *41*
flog *29*
flood *75*
floor *98*
flop *99*
floss *16*
flounce *16*
flour *111*
flow *100*

flowed *94*
flower *111*
flown *14*
flows *80*
flu *129*
flue *128*
fluff *88*
flume *95*
flung *70*
flush *97*
flute *15*
fly *110*
flyer *38*
foal *50*
foe *100*
foes *80*
fog *29*
foil *81*
fold *82*
folk *81*
fond *85*
fondue *128*
food *40*
fool *86*
football *119*
footprint *87*
for *98*
forbid *67*
ford *69*
forever *33*
forgave *20*
forget *60*
forgot *87*
fork *107*
forlorn *22*
form *104*
fort *103*
fortune *75*
fought *103*
foul *83*
found *96*
four *98*
fourteen *89*

fowl 83
fox *41*
fragile 100
fragment 108
frail 106
frame 76
France 27
frank 11
frantic 89
fraught 103
fray 124
frayed 101
freak 102
free 112
freed 120
freeze 42
frequent 108
fret 60
friar 38
fridge 16
fried 92
friend 33
friendship 128
fries 123
fright 68
frill 58
frock 65
frocks 41
frog 29
frogspawn 22
front 55
frontier 32
frown 112
frowned 96
froze 80
fruit 15
frump 61
frustrate 45
fry 110
fryer 38

fuel 86
fulfil 58
full 88
fumble 96
fume 95
fun 105
funny 52
fur 44
furious 115
furl 46
fuse 116
fuss 115

G

gadget 60
gag 39
gain 90
gale 106
galore 98
game 76
gang 10
gap 71
gape 46
gargoyle 81
gash 24
gate 45
gave 20
gawk 107
gear 32
gel 120
gene 89
genie 112
genius 115
get 60
ghost 86
ghoul 86
gig 12
gill 58
gimmick 89
gimmicks 74
girl 46
glad 27
glance 27

gland 48
glare 8
glass 46
gleam 29
glean 89
glee 112
glen 49
glide 92
glint 87
glitch 59
gloat 20
globule 86
gloom 95
glorious 115
gloss 16
glove 70
glow 100
glowed 94
glower 111
glows 80
glue 128
glued 40
glug 61
glum 75
glut 55
gnash 24
gnat 49
gnaw 98
gnu 129
go 100
goad 94
goal 50
goat 20
gob 61
goblin 122
goes 80
gold 82
gondolier 32
gong 101
good 54
goodbye 110
goosebump 61

gore 98
gorgeous 115
gossip 128
got 87
gown 112
grab 23
grace 34
graced 85
graceful 88
grade 101
graffiti 112
grain 90
gram 60
gran 117
grand 48
grape 46
grass 46
grate 45
gratitude 40
grave 20
greased 33
great 45
greed 120
Greek 102
green 89
greet 72
Greg 67
gremlin 122
grew 128
grey 124
grid 67
griddle 73
grill 58
grim 105
grime 111
grin 122
grind 36
grip 128
grit 49
groan 14
grog 29
groom 95

grope 96
ground 96
group 54
grow 100
growl 83
grown 14
grows 80
grub 47
gruff 88
grumble 96
grunt 55
guarantee 112
guaranteed 120
guard 126
guess 30
guessed 118
guest 118
guffaw 98
guide 92
guise 123
guitar 18
gum 75
gun 105
guru 129
gush 97
gust 30
gut 55
guy 110
gym 105

H

ha 18
habit 49
habitat 49
hack 13
had 27
hag 39
ha-ha 18
hail 106
hair 8
hairy 48

hall 119
halo 100
ham 60
hand 48
handcuff 88
hang 10
happiness 30
hard 126
hardship 128
hare 8
hark 28
harm 10
harmful 88
harpoon 75
hash 24
haste 85
hat 49
hatch 19
hate 45
haul 119
hawk 107
hay 124
haystack 13
he 112
head 91
headache 66
heal 122
heap 63
hear 32
heard 12
heart 19
heat 72
heatwave 20
hedgerow 100
heed 120
heel 122
height 68
heirloom 95
hell 120
hello 100
hello 127
helmet 60

helpless 30
hen 49
her 44
herd 12
here 32
hero 100
herself 33
hey 124
hiccup 114
hid 67
hide 92
hideous 115
hideout 83
high 110
higher 38
highs 123
high-tech 78
hijacked 8
hike 12
hilarious 115
hill 58
him 105
himself 33
Hindu 129
hint 87
hip 128
hippo 100
hippopota-
  mus 115
hire 38
hiss 65
hissed 74
hit 49
hitch 59
hive 39
hoard 69
hob 61
hobnob 61
hoe 100
hoes 80
hog 29
hold 82
hole 50

holiday 124
honey 52
honeymoon
  75
honey 112
hood 54
hook 21
hoop 54
hooray 124
hoot 15
hop 99
hope 96
hopeful 88
horde 69
horn 22
horoscope
  96
horrendous
  115
horrified 92
horrifies 123
horrify 110
horseback
  13
hose 80
host 86
hostile 100
hot 87
hotel 120
hound 96
hour 111
house 54
how 23
however 33
howl 83
hub 47
hubbub 47
hue 128
hues 116
huff 88
hug 61
hullaballoo
  128

hum 75
humble 96
hump 61
humpbacked
  8
hunch 70
hung 70
hunk 113
hunt 55
hurl 46
hurray 124
hurt 99
hush 97
hut 55
hygiene 89
hymn 105
hypnotize
  123

I
I 110
ice 56
icecream 29
icicle 109
I'd 92
ideal 122
idolize 123
igloo 128
ignite 68
ignore 98
ignored 69
ill 58
I'll 100
I'm 111
imp 59
impact 8
impale 106
import 103
impress 30
impressed
  118
in 122
include 40

increased 33
indeed 120
indoor 98
inept 26
infest 118
ingenious
  115
inhale 106
ink 59
inn 122
inner 29
inquire 38
inside 92
insist 74
inspire 38
instead 91
intend 33
intercept 26
internet 60
interview
  128
intrude 40
invade 101
invent 108
invest 118
investigate
  45
invite 68
irritate 45
isle 100
it 49
itch 59
itself 33
I've 39

J
jab 23
jack 13
jackdaw 98
jacket 60
jackpot 87
jade 101
jaguar 18

jail 106
jam 60
jamboree
  112
Jane 90
Japan 117
jar 18
jarred 126
javelin 122
jaw 98
jealous 115
Jean 89
jeep 63
jeer 32
jest 118
jet 60
jig 12
Jill 58
Jim 105
jive 39
job 61
Joe 100
jog 29
joke 81
jot 87
joy 112
joyful 88
jubilee 112
jug 61
juggernaut
  103
July 110
jumble 96
jump 61
June 75
junk 113
just 30
jut 55

K
kangaroo
  128

kangaroos
  116
Kate 45
kayak 13
kebab 23
keel 122
keen 89
keep 63
keg 67
Ken 49
kept 26
kettle 78
key 112
keyboard 69
keys 42
kick 89
kicks 74
kid 67
kidnap 71
kill 58
Kim 105
kin 122
kind 36
kindness 30
king 64
kink 59
kip 128
kiss 65
kissed 74
kit 49
kite 68
knack 13
knave 20
knead 120
knee 112
kneel 122
knees 42
knelt 12
knew 128
knight 68
knit 49
knob 61
knock 65

raw 98
ray 124
reach 11
react 8
read 91
read 120
real 122
realize 123
reap 63
rear 32
rebel 120
reboot 15
recent 108
recipe 112
recite 68
recline 79
recognize 123
recoil 81
recommend 33
record 69
red 91
redeem 29
reed 120
reek 102
reel 122
referee 112
refereed 120
referees 42
refrain 90
refugee 112
refuse 116
regard 126
regret 60
rehearsed 39
reign 90
rein 90
released 33
relent 108
rely 110
remain 90
remark 28

remind 36
remote 20
rendezvous 129
renowned 96
rent 108
repair 8
repeat 72
replace 34
replaced 85
replies 123
reply 110
report 103
reptile 100
request 118
rescued 40
resent 108
resign 79
resist 74
resort 103
respond 85
rest 118
restaurant 10
retreat 72
return 115
reveal 122
revere 32
revise 123
revive 39
revue 128
reward 69
rewind 36
rhyme 111
rice 56
rich 59
ricochet 124
rid 67
riddle 73
ride 92
ridge 16
ridicule 86
rig 12

right 68
rigid 67
rim 105
rind 36
ring 64
rink 59
rip 128
rise 123
river 93
road 94
roar 98
roared 69
roast 86
rob 61
robin 122
robot 87
rock 65
rocket 60
rocks 41
rode 94
rodeo 100
role 50
roll 50
rolled 82
rook 21
room 95
root 15
rope 96
rose 80
rot 87
rote 20
rough 88
round 96
rout 83
routine 89
row 23
row 100
rowed 94
rows 80
Roy 112
royal 81
rub 47
rubbish 39

rubble 17
rucksack 13
rude 40
rue 128
rug 61
ruin 122
rule 86
rum 75
rumble 96
rump 61
run 105
rung 70
runny 52
runt 55
ruse 116
rush 97
rust 30
rut 55

S
sachet 124
sack 13
sacked 8
sacrifice 56
sad 27
sag 39
sage 84
said 91
sail 106
saint 85
sake 66
saloon 75
salute 15
Sam 60
same 76
sand 48
sane 90
sang 10
sank 11
sap 71
sardine 89
sarong 101
sash 24

sat 49
satin 122
satisfy 110
save 20
saw 98
sawn 22
say 124
scab 23
scaffold 82
scale 106
scam 60
scamp 104
scan 117
scanned 48
scant 10
scar 18
scare 8
scarecrow 100
scarred 126
scary 48
scene 89
scent 108
schedule 86
scheme 29
school 86
scold 82
scoop 54
scoot 15
scope 96
score 98
scoreboard 69
scored 69
scorn 22
Scot 87
scour 111
scout 83
scowl 83
scram 60
scrap 71
scrape 46
scratch 19

scrawl 119
scream 29
screech 11
screen 89
screw 128
screwed 40
screws 116
scrimp 59
scroll 50
scrub 47
scruff 88
scrum 75
scrunch 70
scud 75
scuff 88
scum 75
sea 112
seal 122
seam 29
seas 42
seat 72
secret 60
see 112
seed 120
seek 102
seem 29
seen 89
seep 63
sees 42
seesaw 98
seize 42
self 33
selfish 39
sell 120
send 33
sent 108
separate 45
sequin 122
serene 89
serious 115
service 65
serviette 60
set 60

settee 112
settle 78
sever 33
severe 32
sew 100
sewn 14
sews 80
shack 13
shade 101
shadow 100
shadows 80
shake 66
shallow 100
sham 60
shame 76
shampoo 128
shampooed 40
shape 46
shard 126
share 8
shark 28
shave 20
shawl 119
she 112
shear 32
shed 91
sheen 89
sheep 63
sheer 32
sheet 72
shelf 33
shell 120
shin 122
shine 79
ship 128
shirt 99
shiver 93
shoal 50
shock 65
shocks 41

shockwave 20
shoe 129
shoelace 34
shoo 128
shooed 40
shook 21
shoot 15
shootout 83
shop 99
shore 98
shorn 22
short 103
shot 87
should 54
shout 83
shove 70
show 100
showed 94
shower 111
shown 14
shows 80
shrank 11
shred 91
shrew 128
shriek 102
shrill 58
shrimp 59
shrine 79
shrink 59
shrub 47
shrug 61
shrunk 113
shun 105
shunt 55
shush 97
shut 55
shy 110
sick 89
sickle 109
side 92
sigh 110
sighed 92

sighs 123
sight 68
sign 79
signed 36
signpost 86
sill 58
sin 122
sincere 32
sinew 128
sing 64
sink 59
sinner 29
sip 128
sir 44
sit 49
site 68
six 74
size 123
skate 45
skateboard 69
skew 128
ski 112
skid 67
skies 123
skill 58
skim 105
skimp 59
skin 122
skint 87
skip 128
skirt 99
skis 42
skunk 113
sky 110
slab 23
slack 13
slam 60
slang 10
slap 71
slapdash 24
slash 24
slate 45

slave 20
sled 91
sleek 102
sleep 63
sleet 72
sleigh 124
slept 26
slew 128
slewed 40
slice 56
slick 89
slid 67
slide 92
slight 68
slim 105
slime 111
sling 64
slink 59
slip 128
slipper 44
sliver 93
slog 29
sloop 54
slop 99
slope 96
slot 87
slow 100
slowed 94
slows 80
slug 61
slum 75
slump 61
slung 70
slunk 113
slur 44
slush 97
sly 110
smack 13
smacked 8
small 119
smart 19
smash 24
smear 32

smell 120
smile 100
smoke 81
smother 17
smug 61
snack 13
snacked 8
snag 39
snail 106
snake 66
snap 71
snare 8
snatch 19
sneak 102
sneer 32
sneeze 42
snip 128
snitch 59
snob 61
snoop 54
snooze 116
snore 98
snored 69
snort 103
snot 87
snout 83
snow 100
snowed 94
snowflake 66
snows 80
snub 47
snuff 88
snug 61
so 100
soak 81
soap 96
soar 98
soared 69
sob 61
sock 65
socks 41
software 8
soil 81

sold 82
sole 50
soled 82
solitaire 8
solitude 40
solo 100
some 75
someone 105
son 105
song 101
soon 75
sore 98
sorrow 100
sort 103
sought 103
soul 50
sound 96
soundtrack 13
soup 54
sour 111
souvenir 32
sow 23
sow 100
sown 14
sows 80
space 34
spaced 85
spade 101
Spain 90
span 117
spank 11
spanned 48
spar 18
spare 8
spark 28
sparred 126
spat 49
speak 102
spear 32
speck 78
sped 91
speech 11